Why We Hunt

Why We Hunt

*The Five Motivations of a
Modern Hunter*

By Aaron B. Futrell

ISBN-13: 9781697910674

Printed in the United States of America

First Printing, 2019

Aaron B. Futrell
413 Riverview St
Canal Fulton, Ohio 44614

Dedication

To my Grandpa, Darl B. Spencer

*The man who taught me how to hunt and
how to live.*

"One does not hunt in order to kill; on the contrary, one kills in order to have hunted...If one were to present the sportsman with the death of the animal as a gift he would refuse it. What he is after is having to win it, to conquer the surly brute through his own effort and skill with all the extras that this carries with it: the immersion in the countryside, the healthfulness of the exercise, the distraction from his job."

-**Jose Ortega y Gasset**, *Meditations on Hunting*

"A downed animal is most certainly the object of a hunting trip, but it becomes an anticlimax when compared to the many other pleasures of the hunt."

-**Fred Bear**

Table of Contents

Preface

"I was not born in the woods, but I got there as soon as I could." I am not sure who first said this quote, but I have heard it a thousand times. And I cannot think of a better statement to describe how I grew up. As far back as I can remember, the forest and the outdoors have always been a part of my life

I grew up in a small town in rural Ohio. We did not have a lot of land, only two acres, but our neighbor gave us free rein of the property behind our house. The cornfields, woods, a creek, and even a nasty swamp were all ours to explore, and we took advantage of it. Looking back, I do not know how many crayfish I caught in that creek or how many forts I built back in the woods. However, what I do remember is all the fun I had. Looking back, I was blessed to grow up in such a place.

Not only did I grow up playing in the outdoors, but I also grew up hunting. Hunting has always been a part of my life. I started at a young age; four years old to be exact, and thirty-plus years later, I have not looked back. For most of my life, I never gave much thought as to why I hunted; it was just something I did. It was not until a few years ago that I started seriously thinking about it.

In college, I studied history. What I found fascinating was how complicated things were. In history, there were no easy answers. Significant events came to be by thousands of smaller events that occurred at just the right time to change the world. But those little events were forgotten; they only reside in the footnotes of history while the significant event remains the focus. I found these small events more exciting.

The best example of this came when I took a class on Colonial America. On the first day of the course, the professor stated that to understand colonial America, you need to start at the beginning, 10,000 BC. For the first few classes, we discussed Native American history and then European History, beginning with the fall of Rome. Finally, after two weeks of classes, we got to Leif Erickson, Christopher Columbus, and the colonization of North America. We were still actually a few weeks away from the American Revolution and actual Colonial America. The reason the class took so long was that not only did we need a foundation of events, but we also needed a foundation of thought. We needed to know all the details to understand it fully.

This class made me realize that people too often simplify things and do not worry about the details. If they want to learn about American colonial history, they go straight to the revolution and skip the little events that led up to it. It becomes a surface level understanding. The same is true about understanding hunting. Most hunters and non-hunters only have a base simplistic knowledge of why they hunt. Only a few have tried to dig deeper into what motivates hunters.

While writing this book, I looked deep into myself and those around me and parsed out our differences, as well as what we had in common. I analyzed these aspects and realized that all hunters have five underlying motivations for why they hunt.

Now this book does not have the exact answers to tell you personally why you hunt, but it will give you the tools you need for deeper reflection into your motivations. I want you to pull back the curtain and take an honest look at yourself. You will discover that you are a complicated being with complicated motives, which cannot be summed up with simplistic titles like "Trophy Hunter" or "Meat Hunter."

So, take a walk with me through my book as I use my years of hunting experience to showcase what motivates us hunters and gives us the desire to pass down our passion to future generations.

Introduction

The History of Hunting

We are all descended from hunters. No one can argue this fact. Every person who lives on this planet is alive today because their ancestors hunted. At some point, someone in their lineage stepped out of their home and into the wild. They killed a living animal and brought it home to eat.

How far back this occurred, however, is different for everyone. Some people do not hunt, but their father or their grandfather did. Others have to go back multiple generations to find a hunter. Maybe there is someone out there whose lineage does not contain a hunter until you get back to the cavemen days, but that is very doubtful.

Hunting dates back to the beginning of time. Arguably hunting is the first profession. I have heard some historians say the first occupation was the prostitute, but they had to be paid with something, and that was probably food. For that reason, I am going to argue that the hunter came first.

In caves all over the world, depictions exist of early man hunting. They show that the tribe's entire lives revolved around hunting. They would follow herds and set up camp near active animal crossings.

Hunting spurred many of the first technological advancements. They started with rocks, then moved on to spears. They invented atlatls to enhance their spears, followed by the bow and arrow. Early man designed many points, knives, and other tools for hunting and processing game. Even one of the first domesticated animals, the dog, was used for hunting.

Hunting was the primary means of acquiring protein for a large part of human history. Even with the proliferation of agriculture and humans raising animals for food, hunting still supplemented peoples' diet.

As we move through time, hunting remained important. The Bible story of Jacob and Esau mentions hunting, as well as, during the Israelites wandering in the wilderness. God sent quail that they caught in nets to eat. Both the Greeks and Romans had gods dedicated to hunting, and many stories in their mythology depict it.

As we move onto medieval Europe, I cannot help but think of the legend of Robin Hood. Even though he is a fictional character, the story shines a light on how that particular society viewed hunting. His very first offense was killing the king's deer. In that time, wild animals were treated the same as domestic. The landowner was the only one who could kill them, or he could sell them. Peasants were severely punished if they were caught poaching, even if they were starving. This attitude would affect how hunting would develop in the New World.

When colonists started crossing the Atlantic to the New World, hunting again became necessary for survival. Deer, turkey, and waterfowl were essential to colonists' survival. But besides survival, hunting played a crucial role in early North American economy. Fur was high in demand and quickly became one of North America's chief exports.

Hunting and the fur trade fueled manifest destiny. The chase for game brought Daniel Boone through the Cumberland Gap and led to the legend of Davy Crocket. Hunting was the fuel that propelled Lewis and Clark to the Pacific and allowed the Mountain Men to brave the dangers of the West.

But during the last half of the 19th-century, hunting turned dark. In many circles, it is known as the market hunting era. Up until this time, many people believed that North America's animal populations were an inexhaustible resource, but that would prove to be untrue.

During this period, species like the passenger pigeon, the eastern elk, and woodland bison would become extinct. Other species were hunted to the brink of extinction. Deer, turkey, bison, and almost every other large animal were gone from most of their native range.

Finally, hunters saw the light. They saw the disappearing game and knew there would be no wildlife left for anyone to enjoy if things continued. This realization started the modern conservation movement. Laws put protections in place, and some types of hunting were banned, while others became strictly regulated. Over the next one hundred years, wildlife rebounded. Whitetail deer and turkey returned to much of their native range. Waterfowl began to flourish again, and many other animals now have a fighting chance for survival.

Today, many believe we are in the golden age of hunting. The land teems with game, and we are experiencing the best hunting in the last 200 years. Wildlife management is at a point where it looks to be sustainable for years to come. But hunting is facing challenges it has never faced before. As wildlife is becoming more abundant, people are becoming less connected to it. Today more people live in urban environments than at any other time in history. This disconnect is affecting the way people view hunting. Many do not see it as needed, and some even see it as immoral. They view hunting as a relic of the past. They are starting to ask, "In this modern world, why do you hunt?"

Throughout this book, I will answer that question and explain the motivations of a modern hunter and why hunting is an honorable and necessary endeavor. I will dive into a few of the most reasons why we hunt and the motivations of the controversial hunting practices and explain why they are still relevant. Join me and discover the modern hunter.

Chapter 1

Why We Hunt

It was the last day of Ohio's second weekend of gun season. I had been unable to hunt the day before, nor was I able to hunt the entire week of gun season that was two weeks earlier. My military obligation had once again gotten in the way of deer season.

I had just driven six hours home from Fort Indiantown Gap, PA and noticed that if I grabbed my gear and left right away, I could make it to my family's hunting property and get in a few hours of hunting. Grabbing my gun and gear and then jumping back in the truck, I drove another hour and a half. Now I was left with two hours of daylight to try and get it done.

There were about six inches of snow on the ground and it was pretty cold, but I did not care. I love hunting in the snow and I could deal with the cold. I tried sitting on one of my stands, but the wind picked up and nearly blew me out of the tree.

The wind made the cold evening even colder, but it did hide the crunch of snow, so sneaking was an option. I decided to still hunt the edges of some known bedding areas hoping to catch a deer moving. For two hours, I snuck through the woods with only seeing the flash of a white tail 200 yards away.

By that time, I was freezing, so I made my way back to the truck. As I was about to cross the road, I saw a doe step out into the field at about 40 yards broadside. The only problem is that she stepped out between me and the neighbor's doublewide. All I could do was watch her cross the road and disappear into the trees on the other side. With that, gun season was over. I would have to wait a few more weeks until muzzleloader season to try and fill my tag.

On the way home, I passed a bank clock and the temperature read -3 degrees. The wind was gusting upwards of 20 knots, so that made the wind chill somewhere around -20 to -30 Fahrenheit. I had been up since 0400 that morning and drove a total of seven and a half hours to hunt two in miserable weather. I looked at myself in the rearview mirror asked myself, "Why do you do this?"

It is a fair question. Why would anyone put themselves through all the pain and misery of a brutal, unsuccessful hunt with seemingly no reward? Why invest all the time and money that goes into hunting? If it is about meat, there are easier ways to get it; for what I paid in gas and time I could have easily bought a steak dinner. So again, I ask, "Why?" What drives a person to hunt?

A few years have passed since that brutal cold hunt and I still ask myself those questions. They have occupied my thoughts and I have tried to make sense of the motivations of why we hunt. I have pondered the reasons why *I* hunt, but why I hunt would not provide a complete answer. I came to realize that other hunters' reasons for hunting are different than mine. What I was really looking for was an overarching answer to why we all hunt.

Even in my circle of hunting buddies, I found that many of the core reasons we all hunt were different. There is no single motive. The answer is complicated and will not be an easy task to break it down into all the intricacies that drives the modern hunter.

The biggest problem I ran into was an oversimplification of the answer. Non-hunters, anti-hunters, and in some cases, even other hunters want to simplify our motivations to fit their own personal ideology. They believe that the motivation to hunt is simple and myopic. This is far from the case.

2

Like any other pursuit, it is multifaceted and many layers deep.

If you ask a dancer why they dance, you will get a multitude of reasons. Some of the answers they give include, but are not limited to, "It's good exercise. It makes me feel alive. It helps me unwind." Plus, I am sure there are tons of other reasons dancers give. Furthermore, it is not just dancers, the same goes for baseball, theater, fishing, and any other pursuit. Humans are complicated, and the reasons that we do different things are also complicated and not always apparent.

Before I get into what hunting is, I want to touch on what hunting is not. I already mentioned that many people see a hunter's motivation as simple. Anti-hunters also want to paint all hunters as having an insatiable bloodlust or that they need to prove they are men or some other simple answer that gives them an excuse to avoid critical thinking. They make the claim that hunters are monsters and that our only desire is to destroy. As any hunter knows, this is far off base. The kill is only a small part of hunting. Sure, it is the goal or climax of the hunt, but to kill is not the primary motivation. If it was the motivation, then hunters have chosen probably the most inefficient way to quench their need for blood.

Hunting, in general, is not an easy endeavor. It takes time, patience, knowledge, and a set of skills that takes many years to hone. Becoming proficient with a bow takes months of diligent practice, the archer will shoot literally thousands of arrows in preparation. And even then just because he can hit a target does not mean he will be a good hunter.

Over the course of a season, a hunter is often more unsuccessful than successful. In a season, I will spend countless hours sitting in a tree stand waiting for perhaps a single opportunity. If it was purely about bloodlust and a desire to kill, there would be much easier ways to kill than hunting.

I remember getting a call from my cousin one afternoon. He had acquired half-dozen live ducks from his in-laws. He had never processed ducks before and even though I was a novice duck hunter, I had cleaned way more ducks than he had, so he asked me to teach him in exchange for half the ducks. I readily agreed since duck is delicious.

The following Saturday he brought over a crate of ducks and we got to work. I had a sharpened hatchet and a log. We methodically took each duck, laid out its neck across the log, and with one swift chop removed the head from the body.

If you have ever heard the phrase "a chicken with its head cut off," I can assure you ducks are just like chickens. They ran around flapping like crazy and made a bloody mess of my backyard. But that was all part of the job. We gathered them up, plucked them, and packaged one each for dinner and the others for the freezer.

Over the course of ten minutes, I had chopped the heads off of all six ducks, which just happens to be the limit of wild duck that I am allowed to kill in a day. Let me tell you, killing those domestic ducks was way easier than killing a limit of wild ones. If it was about blood and killing, I know which way I would go.

Honestly, I did not get a thrill from killing those ducks. The butchering was a job that needed to be done. I processed them from living creatures into food. Do not get me wrong, I was happy to have three ducks to eat and got some satisfaction on being self-reliant, but I would not call the job exciting.

On the other hand, if I had killed a limit of mallards, I would be beyond thrilled, even ecstatic. So, what is the difference? The difference is wrapped up in the ancillary things that go into a hunt. I do not have a long drive to butcher ducks. I could easily raise ducks, chickens, or any other domestic livestock and kill to my heart's content. I could rack up a serious body count with little effort. But hunting is not all about the kill; there is way more to it.

Another simplistic view of hunting says it is about trying to prove you are a man. Many like to cite "trophy hunting" as proof. They say most hunters are only after horns, antlers, and other mementoes to prove their virility. The hanging of heads on a wall and the posting of dead animals to social media only solidify this point of view.

The term trophy hunting has become loaded over the last decade, and it comes with it a stereotypical picture of what a trophy hunter is and how he behaves. The picture that is painted is a rich white guy who desires to kill everything in his path without regard to anything else but himself. That picture is easy to paint. The hunters pay exorbitant amounts of money to chase after lions, elephants, rhinos, and a plethora of other game. Most do not take the meat home with them after their safari but donate it to locals. The simple way to explain it is that it is just about the kill and the ego that it feeds.

I already touched on how it is not all about the kill, but let me explain what is behind the hunting trophy and try and answer these questions: Why do hunters put dead animals on the wall? Why do they take pictures of themselves with their kill? If it is not about ego, what is it?

One of my friends climbed Mount Kilimanjaro a few years back. At the top of the mountain, he took a picture of himself next to the sign announcing his accomplishment. After coming down off the mountain and finding an internet connection, the first thing he did was post that picture. It is a simple picture of my friend standing on some rocks next to a sign. What caused him to first take that photo, and then what motivated him to post it?

That picture represents his whole journey, even though we only see him at his goal. It does not show the months of training to build up the endurance to make the climb. It does not show the hours it took to plan the trip. And it does not show the journey up the mountain or the journey back down. But every time he looks at it, he sees those things.

He sees the training, planning, and the journey. To him, they are all present in the picture, which represents the culmination of hard work and planning which ultimately led to a great achievement.

Our hunting pictures and trophies are the same way. They show us smiling over our dead deer, elk or moose. They don't show the hours of shooting, the time we spent scouting, the long hours in the tree stand, or even the work it takes to break a carcass down into meat. None of that is in the picture. But as hunters, we see it. And just like my friend's picture, to us it represents the culmination of hard work and planning. This is why hunters show their "trophy".

It is not all about ego, but a way to preserve the memory of the hunt. A picture paints a thousand words, but ten thousand more are needed to show what the trophies actually mean and represent.

Our motivations to hunt are complicated and cannot be summed up in simplistic terms. We do not hunt out of bloodlust. We do not kill for fun. Nor is it simply for a trophy. We seek adventure, time in nature, and self-sufficiency. It is about the journey and the fulfillment of providing yourself with food afterward. Do not get me wrong, the kill is the goal, but it is not the complete picture. I want to dig deep and discovered what motivates a person to put themselves through pain and discomfort and spend tons of money to do an activity that some consider obsolete.

Perhaps the greatest revelation in thinking about this topic came when I realized there is no overarching reason why people hunt, but I believe that a hunter's motivations fall into not one, but five broad categories. It is my goal to lay out these categories and explain how they work in concert with one another making up an individual hunter's motivation, and ultimately, answer the question, Why We Hunt?

Chapter 2

The Five Motivations

Imagine your perfect hunt. It does not matter what it is. You are a master of the universe. It can be any animal, any time of year, any season. Whatever you want. If you could lay out the perfect hunt, what would it be? Who would you go with? Where would you hunt? Would it be dangerous game in Africa, caribou in Alaska, Idaho elk, or maybe Midwest whitetail?

I can think of a lot of hunts that I would love to go on. There are many different animals I would love to pursue, and tons of places I would like to see. Wild pigs, caribou, and moose are near the top of my bucket list, but there is one hunt that tops them all. I have lived this hunt many times over in my mind, and I cannot wait for it to be a reality.

For me, that dream hunt is doing a backcountry hunt in Montana. They have what is called the Sportsman's tag which allows for a non-resident hunter to kill one deer and one elk. What I want to do is get an outfitter to drop my brother, my cousin, and myself at a spike camp and leave us there for the next ten days and let the adventure begin. Like I said, I have already planned this hunt out in my mind and have killed many imaginary mule deer and elk. I know the real experience will be different, but that's what dreams are for.

I imagine we would wake up way before first light and position ourselves on a high lookout. The sun would start peeking out from behind the horizon, and the world would begin to stir. We would see the massive valley spread out before us with a mixture of grasslands and timber. We would hear birds chirping with the occasional interruption of an elk's bugle.

Right below us, a herd of elk step out from a stand of trees and feed right towards us. It is a group of cows along with a massive 6x6 bull. They close the distance to within 100 yards. The bull clears the cows, and I tuck a bullet right behind the front shoulder. The mighty elk crumples to the ground as his cows scatter.

For the rest of the ten days, we feast on elk as we methodically explore the rest of the surrounding country. We hunt long and hard and are blessed to fill our tags. Well, all except for my cousin Stephen, he misses a giant bull with his recurve, and we get to give him hell the rest of the trip.

When the hunt is over, we come home completely exhausted, but completely satisfied with the successful hunt. We get to share the meat and adventures with the rest of our family and friends. It is the type of hunt that will live forever in our memories.

I think that for most hunters, that type of hunt would be a dream come true, or if you have done it, an awesome memory. It would be the gold standard of pursuits, and the memories will last a lifetime. One of the reasons a hunt like that would be so special is because it incorporates all five of the motivations: Meat, Adventure, Camaraderie, Challenge, and Spirituality.

You have the adventure of hunting a new place without knowing what is over the next ridge. The challenge comes from trying to outwit a new species in an unfamiliar location. All while being immersed in scenery that takes your breath away and shows the power of an almighty Creator. The successful hunt means meat that you can enjoy for months to come and being able to share the whole adventure with great company.

When I decided on the categories, I made them broad on purpose. You need broad categories to encompass everyone's motivation. While these categories are still complicated, there is some overlap. Breaking it up into smaller pieces is the best way I see to answer the question of why we hunt.

Let me break the Categories down for you. I will talk about each one in-depth in the coming chapters, but I want you to get a good feel for them before we discuss how they work.

Meat: It is about filling the freezer. It is a simple motivation – shoot animals, get food. It is the original motivation for hunting, acquiring meat to feed one's self and one's family. It is not a complicated motivation but a critical one.

Adventure: It is the story and the journey that is important. You do not even have to make a kill to have a successful hunt as long as you have a great time doing it. You are driven by what is over the next ridge or what is going to happen if you sit one more hour. The mystery of the unknown is enticing.

Camaraderie: It is all about who you hunt with and the memories you make. It includes sharing in another's kill as well as being back at camp sitting around the fireplace. It is about spending time with your kids or going hunting one last time with your dad. Hunting is about the memories that last a lifetime and with whom you share them.

Challenge: Anyone who has ever hunted knows it is not easy, and that is what drives some hunters. The sense of accomplishing a hard task can be like a drug. To keep getting that high, some hunters restrict themselves. Examples include restricting your equipment such as using a bow or even dropping down to a stick bow. Others only chase after a specific size animal. The harder you make the hunt, the sweeter victory tastes.

Spirituality: It is about being in nature and feeling a connection to the land. Hunting offers us a chance to be part of nature, not just an observer. Whether you believe in God or not, it is hard to deny the power of nature and a connection you feel when you immerse yourself in it. That feeling drives hunters to get up early and stay late, so they do not miss any part of such a fantastic world.

As you read through the list, you can start to see that you have these motivations. Some of you may even be able to point out exactly which one is the strongest. What you will come to understand is that you are your unique mix, and it is this mix that makes you an individual hunter with individual motivations. All the motivations work in concert to make you who you are.

We are the sum of our parts. I believe all hunters have all five motivators but in differing quantities. I would also postulate that most hunters have a primary motivator that is the main drive to why they hunt.

The best example of how this works comes from a completely unrelated book that I am sure some of you are familiar with, *The Five Love Languages* by Gary Chapman. The book outlines five ways humans show love. They are: Words of Affirmation, Acts of Service, Receiving Gifts, Quality Time, and Physical Touch. A person engages in each of these love languages while in a relationship. They are arranged hierarchically with some being more important to the individual than others.

For me, my primary love language is physical touch. It does not mean I do not like spending quality time with my wife or dislike receiving gifts. It just means that the absolute most meaningful way for my wife to show me she loves me is a hug, kiss, or well, you know what I mean. My wife's primary love language is acts of service. She appreciates and loves when I do things for her. By knowing each other's love language, we can communicate our love more effectively. This knowledge builds understanding among us and makes our marriage stronger.

This concept is similar to why I am writing about the five motivations of a hunter. I seek to help hunters understand each other and build a more united front to deal with future challenges that the hunting community will face. I came up with this list after talking to a lot of hunters in person or on the web. Many only know why *they* hunt and cannot comprehend that others may hunt for a different reason.

Social media is a blessing and a curse. A lot of people, myself included, spend way too much time on Facebook, Instagram, or some other platform when we could be getting something worthwhile accomplished. The good part about it is that it is a great way to spread information and get an idea of how people think about any given topic.

It has helped me immensely with research for this book. I do not know if I would have been able to write this without the observations that have come from social media. It provides a good look into what is going on it any particular community. Social media emboldens people, and they are more likely to express themselves online rather than in person.

The conversations and posts I have read on Facebook have been the driving force in trying to figure out what our motivations are. Some posts have been encouraging and others not so much. I have come to understand that hunters run the gamut on what motivates them, and how short-sighted some are when it comes to another's motivation. A little understanding goes a long way in building allies.

I remember reading a Facebook post from a fellow hunter complaining about "Meat Hunters." The premise of the post was something like, "If you're a meat hunter, why don't you just shoot does and leave the bucks for us, trophy hunters?" This hunter was viewing the motivations of the other myopically and reduced his complex motivations to a simple us vs. them argument. This type of thinking does nothing but incite anger and resentment. Meat hunters and trophy hunters can get along, and all it takes is a little understanding.

For me, the most important reason why I hunt is meat. My cousin, Stephen, on the other hand, would instead pass on a doe or smaller buck to shoot a mature deer. It is not that he does not like deer meat; he loves it, but he places a higher priority on the challenge of the hunt than filling the freezer. (And because of this he has not killed a deer in the last two years.)

However, we both love meat, and we both love antlers. The difference comes in which one does our primary motivation lie. I would instead fill my tag every year and have meat. Stephen would be ok with eating tag soup every few years if that meant him harvesting a mature buck.

My plan every hunting season is to shoot a doe as quickly as I can and get meat in the freezer. Then I will have the motivation to sit and wait on a nice buck. The challenge of the hunt is a secondary motive. After I have meat in the freezer, my motivation becomes more like Stephen's.

Now that does not mean I will shoot a little fork horn early in the season. In Ohio, we only get one buck, so I had better make it count. But as the season wears on and I do not have meat, my standards begin to drop, like a desperate college student at a bar. He starts out hitting on the eights, nines, and tens but by the end of the night, he is willing to shoot a spike, if you know what I mean.

Conversely, when Stephen shoots a mature buck and fills his one buck tag does that mean he stops hunting? No, he goes out again and tries to fill a couple of doe tags. Why? Because he wants to put more meat in the freezer. He becomes more like me, without the temptation to shoot a smaller buck. So even though our motivations are different, we understand each other. We may talk crap to each other, but at the end of the day, we respect each other's motivations and how we decide to hunt.

We all have a different hierarchy of motivations. They are what make us unique as hunters and people. The key is to try and understand why other hunters hunt the way they do and why you hunt the way you do. This shared understanding will build tolerance and strengthen the future of hunting. Remember, a little knowledge goes a long way.

Meat

Chapter 3

My grandpa, before he passed away, used to tell stories about growing up in the small town of Junior, West Virginia. He was a great storyteller, and most of his stories revolved around hunting, and fishing. There is a good reason for this because his family was one of the poorest in town, and if his family ate meat, it was because either my grandpa or his dad, my great-grandpa, shot it.

There were not a lot of deer in West Virginia in the 1930s, and 1940's when he grew up, so most of his time was spent chasing small game. He would hunt squirrels, rabbit, and grouse, as well as trap furbearers to pay for shotgun shells.

My grandpa was a modern-day mountain man, and it all started at a young age. My great-grandma told me the story about the first time he brought home meat. He was three. He had been playing down near a fence in the front yard, and a groundhog happened to come by. As near as my great-grandma could figure out, he found a branch and somehow managed to whack it over the head multiple times killing it. She said she saw him coming back up to the house dragging the groundhog behind him. It was nearly as big as him. That evening they ate groundhog for dinner, and it was the first of many meals my grandpa would provide for his family. He kept his family alive, especially when his dad was drafted into the Navy during World War II. He became the sole provider of meat for the entire time my great-grandpa was fighting the Germans. Getting meat was his job.

If he located an animal, he would not give up until it was in his game bag. He told me if he found a squirrel late in the evening and it got into a hole before he could get a shot, he would wake up extra early the next morning and camp out underneath the tree and shoot him as soon as the squirrel poked its little head out of the tree.

He used to carry a strand of barbed wire with him while rabbit hunting. If a rabbit got down a hole, he would push the wire down the hole and twist. The barbed wire would get twisted up in its fur, and he would be able to pull the rabbit out. If the barbed wire did not work, he would smoke them out. If the hole had multiple entrances, he would stop all of them up but the entrance hole. He would then build a fire near the hole's opening and direct the smoke down it. Before long, the rabbit would not be able to take the smoke, and it would run out the unstopped hole, and he would have an easy shot. Meat was the most crucial reason my grandpa hunted.

As deer populations grew, so did my grandpa's love for chasing them. He figured that one kill would provide enough meat for multiple meals, instead of the one meal a rabbit or squirrel would give. Deer became his passion, and he would chase them every fall.

He was probably one of the greatest deer hunters the world has ever seen. Till this day, he has killed more deer than any person I have ever known. He killed some nice bucks throughout the years, but the genuinely massive trophy always eluded him. I believe the reason had to do with his upbringing.

If he had a tag in his pocket and a legal deer walked by, he would fill it. He could not pass up the meat. He could not bring himself to let a one and a one and a half-year-old buck walk, because that deer meant food and all growing up his family counted on him to provide. I guess old habits die hard.

Today, most hunters do not hunt for subsistence; most have the option of getting meat from a grocery store. If I stopped hunting today, my family would not starve. Our survival does not depend on what I bring home from one of my hunting trips, but that does not mean hunting is obsolete. Wild game meat still helps with the grocery bill. I can put a few deer in the freezer along with the quarter beef we buy every year, and my family does not need to purchase red meat for an entire year.

I know some people will say that the amount hunters spend on hunting negates any cost savings for what meat you get from hunting. I would say that depends. I do not buy a new bow, new hunting clothes, or a ton of gimmicks every year like some hunters. I try to keep my gear as economical as I can and still be successful.

Every year hunting gets cheaper; take my shotgun, for instance. I spent $500 on it over 15 years ago, and I have killed a couple of dozen deer along with numerous squirrels, rabbits, and ducks, I have lost count. The cost of my shotgun equates to cents per pound of meat. And with every kill, it gets a little more cost-effective.

I also figure if I did not have hunting, I would have some other hobby to occupy my time. At least with hunting, I have the chance to bring something home. You cannot say that about golf. The money you spend to play a round of golf ends with literally nothing to show for it. At least with hunting, you have a chance to recoup some of your expenses.

Plus, you cannot compare wild game meat to the meat you find in the store. If I were to buy comparable meat, it would cost a ton. Wild game is organic and free-range. Sure, it may not be certified, but it the most natural meat you can buy. Trust me, the meat you get while hunting is not the cheap cuts you can get at your local grocery store. The meat hunters get properly is high quality. I shot a mallard and cooked it up with a maple bourbon glaze. If you were going to buy a similar dish at a restaurant, you would pay upwards of twenty bucks. In my humble opinion hunters eat like kings.

Wild game meat has also started a sort of food renaissance. More people are getting into the sport to not only have access to high-quality meat, but to have a greater connection with their food. They want to know where their food comes from and that it lived a good life. They want the peace of mind that you cannot get from meat packed in cellophane that sits in your grocery store's shelf.

For adults that start hunting for the first time, meat is the number one draw. It is tangible, and acquiring it naturally makes sense to a lot of people. They look at the factory farm system we have and come to the realization that it is not normal.

There are only three ways to remove one's self from the meat factory system. The first is to go vegetarian and give up meat entirely. The second way is only buying meat from small sustainable farms. And the third is hunting. For most of the population, going vegetarian is not an option, so that directs people to the other two options. Some pick one or the other, and some do a combination of both.

Not only does meat bring others into the sport, but it also makes people who will never hunt, hunter friendly. I do not know how many times I have shared wild game meat with non-hunters. I like to call it chili and jerky diplomacy. Those two dishes seem to be the non-hunting public's gateway drug into the world of wild game.

I share my game meat whenever possible. I think part of the reason goes back to how we developed as humans. It is ingrained in us to share our success with the rest of the tribe. They celebrate a successful hunt, and part of that celebration is sharing it with others. There is a little bit of self-gratitude to go along on with it. The sharing of meat is the ultimate, "look at me; look at what I provided". As humans, we like that. It makes us feel important and appreciated. Back in the caveman days, it would also help with social status. The one who provides the meat would get an elevated position in society, especially if you did it consistently.

Even people that do not hunt realize how special game meat is. If I bring in beef jerky to work, people will take it because it tastes good; however, if I bring in deer jerky it is different. They know it is something special. It is something that they cannot get just anywhere and that it is in a limited quantity. It holds a higher place in the snack food hierarchy then plain old beef jerky.

For a lot of those reasons, even I hold wild game meat to a higher standard, especially when it came from an animal I killed. It gives me a more personal connection to that meat and therefore a greater appreciation for it. I know what went into getting it. It took effort, patience, and was not easy.

I have killed many animals, and I have seen their life force ebb out of their body. It is a powerful thing to witness. They die so I can live, and every time I eat that meat, I see the animal and appreciate its sacrifice. It is not the sort of thing that I take lightly. I know that I am responsible for that life I took, and with that responsibility comes a particular obligation. I like to call it the "Hunters Obligation," and it has to do with taking care of and cooking the meat in the best way possible.

The hunter is obligated to treat the meat with the utmost respect. The hunter took the animal's life, and needs to see that it was not killed in vain. I believe this goes far beyond not wasting it. I want to give it the most honor I can, by cooking it the best way I know-how.

21

Meat is hunting's greatest ambassador. I could spend hours trying to explain to a non-hunter why I hunt, or I can present him with a perfectly cooked deer loin. I know for a fact the loin will speak clearer than I could. With food, I have given several non-hunters a more favorable view of hunting. Some are a little reluctant at first, but if it is prepared well, most come around and try it. And the better you can make it, the better ambassador it is.

Meat is a powerful motivator, and it ranks very high for all hunters in their motivation matrix. I do not know any hunter personally that does not love having their freezer full at the end of hunting season. I have heard rumors of hunters that do not use the meat, but even those hunters do not let it go to waste. They make sure that other people's freezers are full, or they donate it to charity.

Meat is probably the primary reason most hunters hunt, and if not, it is perhaps second or third on the list. I would go as far as to say that the meat aspect is what keeps hunting alive. It is the part of killing that non-hunters readily understand and accept. But even though meat is number one on the list and it is crucial to the future of hunting, it is not the only reason people hunt. The other four aspects also play a role in painting the entire picture.

Adventure

Chapter 4

I grew up hunting with my grandpa in the mountains of West Virginia. One particular year when I was a teenager, my grandpa wounded a buck. He shot low and broke its leg. At that point, everything stopped, and the entire hunting party focused on getting that buck.

My grandpa would follow the blood trail while his brother, my great-uncle, directed us to locations in an attempt to get in front of the deer, so when it jumped out, we could hopefully put it down. We chased that deer all day and finally near dark my great uncle jumped it out of bed and put the finishing shot on it.

When grandpa walked up to him, they knew they were in a predicament. State law dictated that the entire deer needed to be taken to a check station, so boning it out and packing it was not an option. So, this deer needed to be taken out whole.

As the crow flies, it was only a few miles from the cabin, but it was all uphill through some of the thickest, steepest, and nastiest country the mountains had to offer. The other option was to drag it downhill off the mountain to the river, which was a good five miles down. There was no easy option on this one.

They decided since it was late, they would field dress the deer, hang him in a tree, and formulate a plan for the morning. We discussed the matter over dinner and decided that downhill was probably the best option. My great uncle, my younger brother, myself, and a guy we called Big Chuck would drag that deer down the mountain, and my grandpa would drive down in his truck and pick us up. Do not ask me how he talked his brother into doing all the hard work; it was his deer. We already knew we had a long hard day ahead of us, but it was about to get even worse. Overnight a warm front pushed in and started melting the four inches of snow. Then came the rain. It turned everything into a nasty slippery mess.

We slipped and slid our way down to the deer. My brother took a nasty fall and gave us a scare, but he seemed alright, and we pushed on. When we got to it, we knew we made the right choice. There was no way we would have been able to drag that deer uphill in that soup. There was no option but to head down the mountain. We took turns dragging. The going was not easy. We trudged through the mud and slick leaves, slipping our way down. Progress was slow.

The first mile took us over two hours, and we knew we still had a long way to go. My uncle decided that the law said the entire deer. It did not say it could not be in pieces. So we quartered the deer up, and all took a section and continued our hike. This decision definitely made it a lot easier, but the going was still rough.

After eight hours, we made it down the mountain, cold, wet, and hungry. And there was my grandpa sitting in a nice warm, dry truck. He was a sight for sore eyes. We jumped in the back of the pickup and headed back up the mountain to camp.

Now that was an adventure. It is stories like that, that drive a person to hunt. In hunting, you never know what can happen. Animals are somewhat unpredictable, and finding, killing, and getting them out of the field can be crazy at times.

The unknown has always been intriguing, and it draws people like a magnet. This idea is consistent in all aspects of human life. Humans naturally have a curiosity, and this causes us to want to explore the unknown. We were created to seek knowledge.

We learn through experience, and we gain knowledge by adventuring into the unknown. This learning can be as simple as exploring a concept in a classroom or as complicated as a trek through the arctic. In a way, they are both adventures. Adventure involves going into the unknown either physically or mentally and coming out the other side with a better understanding of how the world works. It leads to knowledge, and history has proven that knowledge is power. The more we know about our world, the more powerful we become.

Hunting is one of the first disciplines that humans applied this concept. Hunters invented new technologies to be more effective at acquiring food. While some of this new technology applied to agriculture, a lot of it became relevant to hunting. Humans invented better spears, tools, traps, and techniques, all to assist them in their taking of game. These new technologies needed testing, and the only way to do that is to take them out into the field and see if they worked. In other words, they needed to go on an adventure to gain knowledge. The hunting grounds were the first laboratories where ideas were tested and perfected, and ineffective approaches were purged.

Humans developed this way, and adventure is part of who we are. It is a motivation for a lot of activities and is an integral part of hunting. It is the quest for adventure that drives a lot of hunters. Whether it is a trek into the unknown wilderness of Alaska or just wondering what can be seen sitting in a tree stand behind the house. The world is a hunter's playground and teeming with adventure.

Hunters are the ultimate participant in nature. When we go afield, we immerse ourselves in it in a way that wildlife watchers, hikers, and other non-consumptive users do not. Hunters morph into a predator and match wits with their query. We must understand them, anticipate their moves, read the terrain, and move through it in a way that does not give up our location.

To be a successful hunter, they must have a laser-like focus and a mind for the small details. They must continuously be reading signs and recalculating their approach. But nature is very unpredictable. Just when you think you have it figured out the unexpected happens, and you are back to square one.

Consistent learning and adapting is all part of the adventure. No hunter has it completely figured out, and that is part of the allure. There is always something to learn and still ways to improve. Hunting is something that will never be completely mastered. The quest for adventure pushes the hunter to explore what is around the river bend or over the next hill. It drives men and women to places that most do not go and allows them to see things many will never see.

Hunting is what caused mankind to populate the earth. Tribes followed herds of game animals across the Bering Land Bridge. They followed them into the unknown with adventure around every corner. In a way, adventure was part of survival. If they did not move with the herds, they would die.

The quest for adventure through hunting has played a considerable role in the formation of the United States and Canada. The fur trade was instrumental in the western expansion, and it attracted men who sought adventure. The wild world seduced these men, and the experience it promised was like a drug. Daniel Boone pushed through the Cumberland Gap seeking the mystical hunting grounds of Kentucky. Boone's love for hunting and adventure ultimately opened up the Ohio River Valley for settlement.

Mountain men, like Jim Bridger and Kit Carson, helped open the West to settlement. They went west to seek adventure and fortune, and hunting and trapping were the vehicles that took them there. They laid the foundation that others would build upon all because of their thirst for adventure and love of hunting.

These men are just a handful of examples that show how adventure and hunting shaped the world where we live. Today there is little left to be explored, but the allure of adventure is still there. Every new piece of ground is its own adventure. Just because it is not unique to mankind does not mean it is not new to me, or that the pull is any less intense.

Modern hunters continuously pay homage to these forefathers of hunting. Hunting, for the most part, is less dangerous than in the past. Hunting is no longer a matter of survival. Therefore, an unsuccessful trip does not mean your family will starve. Most hunters could get what they need from the grocery store, but it is not the same. A trip to the butcher's counter does not satisfy the urge that dwells deep inside us.

Challenge

Chapter 5

There is a reason why they call a recurve bow the "struggle stick." It is challenging to become consistent and extremely hard to master, and that is just target shooting. When you add in the rigors and unexpected nature of hunting, it makes being a successful hunter with a recurve or longbow extremely difficult.

My cousin, Stephen, is a capable hunter. Not counting the last two years, he had a successful hunting streak of at least ten seasons where he killed either one or more whitetail deer. Over the previous two seasons, he has put up big goose eggs. All because he decided he wanted to try and kill a deer with a recurve.

In the last few years, his primary focus has been on the challenge of hunting. I think he is doing it for two reasons. First, he loves a challenge and strives for excellence. Secondly, he is a little bit of a jerk and wants to be able to talk trash to the others in our hunting group. He figures if he can successfully kill a deer with a recurve, it would mean that he is the better hunter, and he will not be shy about letting us know.

One thing about hunters who are motivated by challenge is that they become obsessive. My cousin shoots hundreds of arrows a week. He has a small shooting range in his basement and he set up a tree stand in his backyard to simulate hunting conditions. If there is something he could do to up his chances, he is going to give it a try. He has been at it for two deer seasons without success, but if you talk to him about it, he tells you his seasons were not unsuccessful. He has seen more deer and learned more about their behavior in the last two years than in his entire 20-year hunting career.

The fact that you need to get a deer within 20 yards and the deer pretty much needs to be in precisely the right spot limits the shot opportunities. He has been able to watch deer and study them. His first year, he learned a few lessons and was able to adapt. I do not think he even let an arrow fly that first year. Any deer he had standing right was not in range, and any deer in range did not give him a clear shot.

For his second year, he changed how he set up his stands, worked on new ways to access his stands, and went extreme with scent control. All of his work paid off because he got the perfect shot at what would have been his largest buck ever. He failed however to factor in one very important basic thing.

My cousin was sitting in his stand right between two bedding areas. The way the hollers come together and a pond on the property makes this a perfect pinch point. Deer crisscross this spot all day long, and during the rut, it is like a highway.

About an hour into the morning sit, he had a decent 9-point come out of the bedding area and cross right in front of him. He was planning on taking the shot at this buck, but something in the buck's behavior told him that something bigger was following him. He was right. Just after that 9-point walked off, out stepped a monster 160-170 class buck and followed the same path of the previous deer. My cousin drew back, and the deer stopped, offering the perfect shot.

Remember, I said he did not account for one thing. That was the wind. We were getting 20 miles per hour wind gusts that day, and the tree he was sitting in was swaying just enough so that when he released the arrow, it sailed over its back by mere inches. The buck took two hops and walked off.

Even though my cousin will never admit it, I believe he sat down and cried. Two years of intense work all come down to a single moment, and not being able to connect was devastating. He came back to the house later that day, and told us the story, and you could see he was sick to his stomach, but he did not let it get him down. He went back out that evening and kept at it.

A few weeks later, I see where he posted a picture of his bow on Facebook with the caption, "For Sale, this bow keeps missing." I asked him about it, and he would not tell me what happened. He said the deer gods gave him the biggest "screw you" ever and he does not want to talk about it. He said it was worse than the story I just wrote about and he is not going to tell anyone what happened until he finally kills a deer with his bow.

Let's face it; hunting is difficult. There are so many variables that have to be taken into account for a hunter to be consistently successful. One little miscalculation can mean the difference between a dead animal, a complete miss, or the worst-case scenario - a wounding shot. Hunting is a hard pursuit, which is the reason why it attracts a lot of hunters. A person gets a lot of personal satisfaction after accomplishing a difficult task. We never remember the easy stuff in life. It is the hard, difficult things that mean the most.

Back in 2015, I completed my first and only marathon while I was deployed to Kuwait. I trained like crazy for two months leading up to it. The race started at 0500 hours, the temperature was already in the 90's, and when I finished four hours and forty-three minutes later it was well over 100 degrees. It was one of the most difficult things I have ever done. A marathon is 26.2 miles, but in reality, it is much longer than that. When you add in the 200 plus miles I ran getting ready for it you begin to see the full picture. I have run countless

5k's and 10k's most of which I cannot tell you my time or even the name of the race, but I will never forget the 2015 Marine Corp Marathon parallel race that took place at Ali Asaleem Air Base, Kuwait. I count it as one of my life's most significant accomplishments.

I set a goal and accomplished it. When it comes to the challenge of hunting it is very much the same. Hunters set goals and try to achieve them. A new hunter's goal might be to kill any deer, while a seasoned veteran might want to increase the challenge by only shooting a deer of a particular age class. This self-imposed restriction is the challenge of the hunt; there are always ways to push yourself to get better and find more personal satisfaction out of the hunt.

There are three main ways that a hunter increases the challenge of the hunt. They all have to do with self-limiting standards. They are in no particular order: type of animal, type of equipment, and hunting method.

Type of Animal – A hunter increases the challenge by the nature of his quarry. Usually, he limits himself to only shoot an animal of a specific size or age. Such as only shooting 3.5-year-old bucks or older, not shooting Jake turkeys, or only shooting male mallards.

Type of Equipment – A hunter increases the challenge by what he uses to kill the animal. Examples are a rifle hunter decides to bow hunt, a bowhunter trades in his compound for a recurve, or a muzzleloader hunter trades in his fancy inline for a flintlock.

Type of Hunting Method – A hunter increases his challenge by how he hunts. Instead of sitting over water for archery antelope, a hunter decides on spot and stalk, instead of jump shooting ducks, he will only shoot decoying birds, or a hunter not use dogs when hunting rabbits and kick the brush himself.

Many hunters use a combination of the three when increasing the challenge. For instance, a hunter whose goal it is to spot and stalk a Pope & Young record book antelope with a recurve bow has a lot more challenges than a hunter whose goal is to shoot any antelope with a rifle.

Sometimes it is the type of animal that offers the challenge. I have never been on a wild sheep hunt, but from what I hear, it is one of the most grueling and challenging hunts in North America. There is a reason that they call getting ready for it, getting "sheep shape."

The same goes for backcountry DIY hunts. They are challenging, especially if they take place in unfamiliar terrain. I am from Ohio and believe me it would be a challenge to strike out into the Bob Marshal Wilderness after elk. I have never hunted elk and also have never been in that environment, but it is a challenge I would love to take on.

A hunt like that would motivate me to get into the best shape of my life, learn all I could about elk, and hone my bushcraft skills to set myself up for success. It would be a challenge and a learning experience, and even if I do not kill an elk, it would be worth it. I would know how to better prepare for the next time and eventually would find success.

Challenge increases patience, perseverance, and skill. If you are going to be a consistently successful hunter, you will need to keep improving in all these areas. These attributes work together to make the hunter the best he can be. As a hunter makes his hunt more difficult, he is forced to increase his skills if he wants to be successful. That is why my cousin has to shoot hundreds of arrows per week. If he did not, he would not have a chance at killing a deer with his recurve.

It is not only skill with your weapon of choice; it also means increasing your woodsmanship and the understanding of your prey. It does not matter how good a shot you are if you cannot locate your quarry; you are not going to be successful.

Perhaps the most essential skills in hunting are the related ideas of patience and perseverance. When I think of patience as it pertains to hunting, I think about the ability to sit in a tree stand on a cold day. You sit past the point of being uncomfortable and willing yourself to sit longer. Knowing that the longer you sit, the better the chance of an animal presenting itself.

Perseverance is related to patience, but I think of it as not just waiting but more of just keeping after it. It is a no-quit attitude. It is recovering from a miss, not giving up, and learning from mistakes. Perseverance is also trying new things and always improving your situation.

All three of these attributes of challenge teaches one to be a better hunter. This concept also translates to other areas of life. The more you challenge yourself, the better person you become. If you take on a hard project and dedicate yourself to mastery, you will gain more knowledge, discipline, and will eventually be a better person than who you were before.

Eventually, my cousin will kill his first deer with a recurve. He will finally taste sweet victory. Even if that is a doe, it is a deer he will remember for the rest of his life. It will be the culmination of literally years of hard work and perseverance.

Hunters that are driven by challenge push themselves, and it ends up being more about the journey and the hard work than the actual kill. For them, nothing comes easy, and they would not have it any other way.

Chapter 6

Camaraderie

When my grandma was getting ready to marry my grandpa, her future mother-in-law, my great-grandma, told her, "If you want to spend time with your husband you need to go get a gun and a fishing pole." My grandma heeded that advice, and it was a recipe for wedded bliss. They were married 49 years until my grandpa died. In those 49 years, they spent a lot of time hunting and fishing.

Not only did my grandma learn to hunt and fish, but she also helped pass that tradition down to her kids. Their whole family hunted. That is how they spent time together.

Every year my grandpa would pack up the entire family and head down from Ohio to West Virginia for deer gun season. They would spend the week hunting as a family. They probably had the most unique hunting camp on the mountain. Back in the 1960s and 1970s, most women did not hunt. But not so in my family. My grandpa had three daughters and two sons, so the family was by majority female, and they all hunted. It is one thing that brought them together.

My grandma is in her mid 80's and she still hunts with us. I know she loves to hunt, and I also know she loves spending time with her grandkids. At times I am not sure which she enjoys more. My brothers, cousins and I sit around the living room of our hunting cabin and talk about some of the most stupid funny things we can think of, and she sits there and takes it all in.

She says it reminds her of my grandpa, his brother, and others they shared hunting camp with back in the day; the way we interact always making jokes, telling stories, and having fun. I think it brings her back to the good old days. She can see her husband's legacy in us, and it gives her joy.

Her family came together around hunting, and it still does to this day. I know without a shadow of a doubt that if it were not for hunting, I would spend less time with a lot of my extended family. Today's world is so busy. The world is always competing for your time, and even though I love my extended family, I know that other priorities would get in the way.

But during hunting season we are all able to come together around a shared past time and take part in each other's lives. We share all the different motivations of hunting I have already mentioned, along with the one I will share in the next chapter. We share in the adventure, the challenge, the meat, and the spiritual aspects of the hunt.

A lot of this can be seen in the relationship between my brother and me. Growing up, we fought like cats and dogs. If I am honest, I would say we both had issues, but since I am talking about my younger brother, I will blame the majority of our fights on him. He was a cocky little punk like most little brothers are, that always tried to fight outside of his weight class. I do not know how many times I had to put him in his place.

Our relationship was not the best. My brother annoyed me to no end, and being the older brother, I did my fair share of tormenting. I am four years older than my brother, so by the time he was old enough to hunt without an adult, I had graduated from high school and shipped off to the Army.

When I returned four years later, a lot had changed. We had both matured (me more than him), and we started hunting together. That is when our relationship started to grow. We would discuss hunting strategies and tactics. We would make plans for the upcoming season and help each other out during the hunt. Today my brother is one of my closest friends, and if it was not for hunting, I know for a fact that we would not be as tight. In all honesty, my brother is a dork. He loves video games and a lot of other stuff that I have no interest in, but hunting brings us together.

One type of hunting, in particular that has brought my brother and I closer is rabbit hunting. It is, without a doubt, some of the most fun hunting there is. Sure, shooting a rabbit is not the high pay off as that of killing a deer, but the hunt itself is so much fun. A lot of people hunt rabbits with dogs, but we do not own dogs, so we have to jump them ourselves by getting in the thickest, nastiest brush in order to kick them out. At the end of the day, if there is not blood on your face from a few stray briars, you were not working hard enough.

Rabbit hunting without dogs is the most camaraderie driven type of hunting there is. Your goal is to scare the rabbits out of their hiding spots, so there is no need to be quiet. Therefore, there is always a lot of talking. Sometimes it is about hunting and other times it is about everyday life. And then comes the talking crap to each other.

Rabbits are also very fast, so when you do jump one out, the shot is almost always challenging. You get the two extremes. You get "great shot" when you hit one, but when you miss, oh boy, you better be ready, because you will be chided and berated until the next rabbit jumps and you either redeem yourself or dig yourself deeper. It is all in good fun, and I would not have it any other way. There is a lot of trash-talking going on but at the end of the day; it is a community hunt. We talk about how many rabbits "WE" got. Sure, there is some individual achievement, but most of the time; your success comes from someone else's work.

A group of us went hunting this past Thanksgiving. I only shot one of the ten rabbits we killed that day, but I jumped a majority of them. Without me going through the nasty thickets, half of those rabbits would have been safe. Rabbit hunting is a team effort, and at the end of the day, we recognize that there is little individual accomplishment; we are only successful as a team.

Another aspect of rabbit hunting that relies on the cooperation and camaraderie of the hunters is the hunt itself. Every thicket is a new hunt and needs its specific plan. There is a conversation about how to best tackle every piece of ground. You set the strategy, execute, and when you get to the next thicket, the planning starts all over. It is essentially pack hunting. It is how hunters have been hunting for thousands of years. Today a lot of hunting is done solo by sitting in a tree stand. But that is not how most hunting historically has taken place. In the past, hunting has always been a group activity.

The movie, *Dances with Wolves,* has perhaps one of the most excellent hunting scenes in movie history. Kevin Costner goes on a buffalo hunt with a group of Sioux Indians. They work together as a team to run and corral the buffalo while on horseback so they can shoot them. Costner distinguished himself in the hunt; he showed his worth and earned a lot of respect from the Sioux. The hunt is a turning point in the movie. Before the hunt, he was not trusted and looked at with skepticism. After the hunt, he starts to be accepted into the tribe. The hunt helped to build the relationship and established trust.

I learned to hunt from my grandpa. He first took me out when I was four years old. We went squirrel hunting at my uncle's property in southern Ohio. I had a little chipmunk .22 that my grandpa carried, and he did his best to try and get me a squirrel. But at four, I could not get it done, but I will forever remember my first hunt.

The next summer, I had turned five, and my grandpa took me out groundhog hunting. Let me tell you, it is a lot easier spotting a groundhog in an open field than it is locating a squirrel up in a tree. Earlier in the spring, my grandpa had me shooting a .222 rifle; it is a gun with a lot of history. If I remember correctly, my mom and at least one of my aunts killed their first groundhog with it, and he wanted to carry on the tradition.

I did not disappoint him. An hour before dark, a big fat groundhog popped his head out of his hole. He had no idea that we were hiding in the tree line. My grandpa positioned the gun in the crook of a tree and gave me the perfect rest, so I placed the crosshairs right on his eye and squeezed the trigger. The gun fired, and the groundhog disappeared.

I thought I missed, but my grandpa knew otherwise, but he did not say a word. We sat there for a few more minutes and got ready to check the hole. Another groundhog came out of the corn next to the alfalfa field we were watching. My grandpa got me set up for the shot and BANG! This time I missed, but we went out to check it anyway. In all of the excitement of the second groundhog, I had forgotten about the first. My grandpa walked up to the hole and told me to look inside. There it was, my first kill, a perfect headshot. I was happy, but my grandpa was excited. I think this hunt marked the beginning of a new path in his life. I was his oldest grandson, and from this point on, he officially had a new hunting buddy.

Over the next 13 years, until I joined the Army, I cannot count the number of hunts we went on. He was with me when I killed my first groundhog, first squirrel, first rabbit, and first deer. Hunting brought us so close. We shared so many memories that when he passed away, I was devastated.

I still think about him daily, but I am comforted by the fact that his legacy lives in me. I am now a father, and I desire to pass his legacy down to my children, along with instilling a legacy of my own. Some of my greatest memories growing up are times I spent hunting with my grandpa, and I want my kids to have those same memories as me.

Hunting has brought my family together and has also brought me closer to friends. For some hunters, this is why they hunt. They love the togetherness and unity. I think some are even content not to be the one that makes the kill, just being there and being a part of the hunt is fine. They love sitting around the fireplace and rehashing the day's hunt. They enjoy planning the next day's activities, who is going to which tree stand, are we going to do a drive, or what do we think the neighbors are doing, and how that affects the deer. They get satisfaction from just being a part of something.

Hunting brings togetherness, unlike any other activity I have experienced. It has helped build my relationships with my family and friends. Every year I look forward to spending time with people I have not seen in a while. The relationships I have developed around hunting are some of the strongest ones in my life.

Chapter 7

Spirituality

I am the world's worst turkey hunter. I have hunted turkeys for 14 seasons and have only killed one Jake. I cannot chalk all of it up to bad luck; I made more than my fair share of mistakes. Let us say I did not have any good luck either. I felt like the good Lord did not want me to get a turkey. I faithfully put in my time for 12 straight seasons (Not counting the year I spent deployed overseas) and had nothing to show for it. If something could go wrong, trust me, it did.

I had turkeys come in and hang up just out of range. Others would come into range but somehow manage not to give me a clear shot. I would decide to move just as a bird was coming in silently behind me and I would scare it into the next county. I made every mistake in the book and sometimes felt like I added a few chapters.

The only bird I was able to harvest came in 2017, after 12 seasons of trying. I was set up with my brother by a couple of ponds. As dawn started to break the entire holler exploded with gobbles, we were in turkey Mecca. Gobblers were coming from all directions. We even saw one sitting on the roost 150 yards away.

As we were watching him gobble, a turkey thundered right behind us. I tried to get turned around, but of course, he saw us. He had walked in without making noise until he was 20 yards away. As he took off, my heart sank. I just blew my only chance for the day and added another chapter to my turkey hunting book of failures.

It was still early, and the gobbler on the roost was still there, so we settled in for the morning. It was not long before we started seeing birds move, but they were all out of range. We adjusted our spot and set up on a clear-cut pipeline. Before long we saw a big tom strut out in the field, where we were sitting moments before. He was all puffed out and could tell he thought he was the king of the valley. That feeling did not last too long as two jakes came out into the field and started a fight. They started chasing this big tom right towards us.

The tom got within 50 yards and took a hard left and ran up into the woods and out of our lives. The jakes seemed satisfied with running him off and started feeding. I hit my box call that got their attention. They headed our way. There was a small tree line between them and us, and they got hung up there, but still definitely in range. I had my gun up as the turkeys looked through the trees and brush trying to find the hen that made the call. One of the birds popped his head into the open, and that was all she wrote.

Boom! I shot, and he started flopping. I jumped up and ran through the tree line and made sure he did not get away. I think I surprised the other bird because he did not fly until I was within five yards of him. When I got there, my bird was still flopping, but he was not going anywhere. After 12 years of trying, I finally had success.

I still consider myself the world's worst turkey hunter, but every year, I count down the days till opening day. Not because of all the success I have, but because turkey hunting offers something no other type of hunting offers. Turkey hunting allows you to get out into the woods well before daylight and wake up with the world. Sure, you can do that with deer hunting, but deer hunting does not take place in the spring. There is something about that time of year that is special. The world is coming alive, and you are part of it.

There is something about sitting with your back against a tree, completely motionless and melting into nature. You become a part of nature and develop a connection with it that you cannot get doing any other activity. You can look across the forest and observe birds chirping, squirrels playing in the new foliage, and a myriad of other animals doing their thing. You can see the complex connections in nature. It truly is one of the things in this world that cannot be described in words. You have to experience it for yourself.

As a religious Christian, I see the world as a beautiful expression of God. I see the wondrous works of His creation and am amazed by the intricacies of the world He designed. It brings me closer to Him.

Psalm 19:1 says, "The Heavens declare the glory of God; the skies proclaim the work of his hands."

Nature was the first scripture God wrote. Before the Bible, we had nature. All of creation is a testimony to how great God is. Everything in nature shows us His power and greatness. He designed everything under heaven with a purpose when He set the world into motion.

This concept is evident in Romans 1:20, "For since the creation of the world God's invisible qualities—his eternal power and divine nature—have been clearly seen, being understood from what has been made, so that people are without excuse."

Being out in nature is one of the ways I connect with God. I read the holy word that is inscribed into the world He created and am inspired to be a better father, husband, and man. It is hard to describe the connection I feel when I spend time in creation, but for me, it is life-changing.

I understand that He appointed us stewards of this world, and it is our job to take care of it and pass it on to the next generation. I believe conservation is a heavenly prescribed duty. God gave us dominion over the animals and of all nature. That does not mean it is ours to exploit, but ours to nurture and grow. We are called to live off the land, but not to its detriment but its benefit. We should treat it with the reverence it deserves and makes it a better place. God has only given us one planet, and we are tasked with maintaining it.

My perspective comes from being a Christian, and I know not everyone shares my religious views. That is fine, because whether you agree with me or not, it does not matter because I know nature speaks. It speaks to the religious and non-religious alike. I have heard many hunters that do not share my religious views talk about the spiritual connection they receive while out hunting. They also connect to nature, and it cleanses the soul and renews the mind just like it does me. They do not equate it to a higher power.

There is no denying that nature is a powerful force, and it is something amazing to be caught up in. In my opinion, hunters experience this spiritual awakening more so than many other outdoor activities. Hunters become immersed in nature more so than hikers, campers, and kayakers, to name a few.

Perhaps the only outdoor activity other than hunting that has a similar immersive quality is wildlife photography. Both are similar in the fact that one must be still and silent and melt into the background and observe the world. We wait, plot, and have to be patient to become successful. After the shutter clicks or the trigger gets pulled, we go our separate ways. The hunter is no longer an observer of nature, but an active participant in the predator and prey dynamics. We take our place in the wild food chain.

If everything goes right, we take a life, and that has its spiritual ramifications. The taking of a life is not something that should be taken lightly.

Stopping another creature's life force is a powerful experience. It changes a person. I have been hunting since I was a kid, but it was not until I was an adult that I truly grasped the implications of killing an animal. I came to terms with taking a life. I understood that it is now my responsibility to make sure it is treated with respect.

When I kill an animal, I have a lot of different emotions; some are even contradictory. I feel happy and sad at the same time. I am delighted that I was successful, that I have meat, and that all my hard work has paid off. On the other hand, I am sad because I love these animals and I am responsible for taking its life. It is a weird paradox that does not make sense unless you experience it.

But above all else, I am thankful; thankful for the meat, the experience, and spiritual renewal. Hunting and being in nature is good for the soul. No matter who you are, you cannot get away from the power nature has. It has spiritual qualities that hunters cannot resist, and for some, the renewal and energy it brings is the main reason hunters keep going out.

It does not matter if a hunter bags his query; just being a part of nature is enough to make a hunt successful. To quote the legendary hunter Fred Bear, "Immerse yourself in the outdoor experience. It will cleanse your soul and make you a better person."

Chapter 8

Balancing the Motives

Over the last few years we have seen quite a number of famous hunters get busted for poaching. You would think that being in the spotlight would create an incentive to keep these guys on the straight and narrow, but that has not been the case. In some cases, I think it has led to the opposite.

In almost all of these cases, the underlying reason can be chalked up to unbalanced motives. These hunters allow their motivations get off kilter and that became a contributing factor that turned them into poachers. They were motivated in such a way that the legality of what they were doing did not matter. Let's take a look two examples of Bill Busbice and Chris Brackett.

Bill Busbice, the founder of Wildgame Nation, had Wyoming's Governor's tag which permitted him to shoot any elk in the state. It did not matter what unit it was in - he could go there and hunt. He found a huge bull and took the shot. He missed the bull but killed a calf elk instead. At this point his hunt should have been over. He had killed an elk and filled his tag, but he kept shooting and killed the bull. To cover up what he had done, he dumped the calf's body in a ditch and tagged the bull. He probably would have gotten away with it, but another group of hunters had witnessed what had happened and reported it to the authorities.

Chris Brackett from the TV show *Fear No Evil*, was on a muzzleloader deer hunt in Indiana. A monster buck walked out, and he shot it, and it ran off. Right after Brackett shot, another bigger buck stepped out, and he quickly reloaded and shot that one as well. In the area he was hunting you are only allowed to kill one buck, so he tagged the bigger buck, and his cameraman tagged the first buck. Video of the incident was leaked, and Brackett was not only hammered in the court of public opinion but charged by the state of Indiana and Illinois.

What these incidents have in common is that they both set the right motives aside and acted in greed and disregard. Their desire for the monster buck or elk came before what was right. They let their motivations get out of balance.

Life is all about balance. You have to balance work and home life, fun and responsibility, spending and saving, and the list goes on. If any one of these things gets out of whack the other side suffers and ultimately, we suffer. The same thing goes for our hunting motivations. They can get lopsided, and at the very least, become problematic, and at the far end illegal or immoral. A hunter needs to maintain a balanced approach to his motivations in order to avoid certain pitfalls.

All of the five motivations that we talked about have the potential for being misused. Sometimes it is an over-abundance of one of the motivations that will get someone into trouble, and sometimes it is the lack of one or more of them that causes the issue. Each one has their own problems when they become unbalanced and it is important to recognize the signs.

Historically, the motivation to acquire meat can become unbalanced through the over harvesting of animals. The market hunting days of the past show us that unfettered meat acquisition can be very problematic. Entire species were wiped out and others were hunted to the brink of extinction because of our quest for meat.

Today, I believe, this has been solved. With the passage of the Lacey Act, it became illegal to sell wild meat, so there is no incentive to over harvest the resource to make a living. The law disconnected the link between wild game and money. This has been beneficial for animal populations all across the country.

Our problem now is the opposite. Some people do not respect meat enough. Have you ever seen a dead deer that has obviously been shot with just the head missing and the meat left to rot? I have seen it a couple of times and each time it makes me furious. For most of the hunting world wasting meat is an egregious violation of ethics and is enough for other hunters to shun the perpetrator.

One of my friends let a guy he worked with hunt his property. The guy ended up shooting a nice 10-point buck. He went up to my friend and said, "I just want the head; you can do whatever you want with the meat." My friend told me that was the last time he was allowed to hunt on his property.

Wasting meat in some states is illegal, and everywhere it should be regarded as immoral. Meat is the best rationale for hunting and the easiest for non-hunters to understand. Purposely wasting meat sets hunting back in the court of public opinion and in the long run could be detrimental to the sport.

You can never have too much adventure, right? Wrong! The quest for adventure becomes problematic when one pushes the limit on what is legal. Some people get a thrill out of breaking the law and see it as an adventure to not get caught. I think this is what motivates a lot of road poachers that shoot deer out of their truck window and then just let the deer lay.

A great example of this is the story of Charles Beaty, who dubbed himself "The Prince of Poachers." He was arrested back in 1998 for poaching 116 trophy whitetail deer over a 22-year period. The story goes, he would sneak onto large trophy ranches in Texas and poach deer. He loved the cat and mouse game he played with game wardens and the property owners. He even wrote a book about his adventures that I refuse to buy. I do not want anyone to profit off of their misdeeds that paint hunting in a poor light.

Hunting is thrilling enough; a person does not need to up the ante by disregarding game laws. If one's regular hunting scenario is not thrilling enough there are better ways of doing it. You could hunt new animals or explore new land. As long as you keep yourself within the limits of the law, it is all good.

The challenge of the hunt can also be misused. One of the ways is not being fully prepared for the challenge. I mentioned before that my cousin is trying to kill a deer with traditional archery equipment. He did not just pick up a recurve, shoot it a few times, and then head out to the woods. He practiced obsessively for months getting ready to hunt. He literally shoots hundreds of arrows a week, so when the time is right, and a deer gives him a shot, he will be able to make a quick, clean kill.

Practice is important for any hunting discipline and knowing your limitations is important. It is also essential not to deviate from them. I know it may be hard not to take a shot at a deer standing at 45 yards when you are only comfortable at shooting 30. It would be very easy to justify; it is only 15 more yards. But you know your limit, and you know at what distances you can make a clean, ethical shot; so, do the right thing and stick to it. The animal you plan to shoot deserves that respect.

Another issue that comes up more often with the challenge motivation is when you start insisting others hunt the way you do. I dedicated an entire chapter of this book to the subject, but I will touch on it briefly. All hunters are different. We all have different goals, desires, and motivations. As long as the activity is legal and ethical, you should have no problem with the way someone else chooses to hunt or what animal they decide is a trophy. We are all at different levels, and we need to encourage each other.

The number one way people abuse camaraderie is by just being a jerk. There was a hunter I used to work with that got upset when he heard anyone had gotten a deer. He would come up to me and say stuff like, "Did you hear so-and-so, got a deer?" He would huff a little bit and you could tell that he was not happy for them. He wanted to be the one killing deer. Sure, I get it, I like killing deer too, but trust me there is plenty to go around. What I always found weird was that he did not even hunt remotely close to where the other guys did, so it was not like they were shooting deer he would even have a chance of killing. I guess he was just bitter.

I want to contrast that story with another. My brother's girlfriend, later ex-girlfriend, went hunting with him down at the farm where we all hunt. It was the last Saturday of shotgun season, and it was her first time out. She ended up shooting the biggest deer of the year and one of the largest ever taken off the property. There could have easily been some jealousy. Many of us that hunt the property could have been upset that "she didn't put her time in" and did not deserve such a nice buck on her first day out. But that was not the case. We all shared in her moment and were excited for her because that is what hunting is all about. We do not need to tear others down in an attempt to build ourselves up. Be happy for each other and celebrate the successes.

The spiritual motivation was the hardest motivation to find a misuse. I think because nature is so pure. Personally, I cannot get enough of it; there is not a thing as too much nature. Well, unless you get eaten by wolves or freeze to death, but those aside, you really cannot overindulge. The issue comes when we take the world around us for granted. Hunters are stewards of the land, and we should leave it a better place. This means cleaning up your spent shell casing, packing out your trash, as well as taking part in conservation programs.

Just like everything in life, a hunter needs to be balanced. He should be cognizant of his motives and keep them in balance. He should not overindulge in some areas and be lacking in others. Just like the golden rule says, we should treat others how we want to be treated and respect the world around us.

This is especially true in the days of social media. Hunters are always being watched. Any action that even has an inkling of being unethical or illegal can and will be blown up in the media. Anti-hunting groups will jump on any impropriety in order to show hunting in a bad light. They highlight the bad actors and use their sins to condemn every one of us. To combat this, we also need to condemn the bad actors within our ranks and distance ourselves from them.

This past year a news story broke that shows my point. One of the most egregious poaching cases I have ever seen was just settled in court and the footage was released. It shows a father and son kill a sow black bear and her cubs while they were in their den. They can be seen celebrating and gloating over their poached trophy. Absolutely, everything the pair did was illegal. It was condemned by not only animal rights activists, but also by hunters. I did not see one hunter try and excuse their behavior.

That did not stop anti-hunting organizations like PETA from trying to castigate all hunters for the actions of the poachers. They did their best to paint the picture that all hunters as blood thirsty killers that have no regard for wildlife or the law. This is absolutely absurd. When we get to the chapter on conservation, I will show you how no one loves and respects animals like hunters.

Poachers and hunters are not the same and have nothing in common. Hunters love and respect wildlife and desire to see it flourish. Hunters understand that game laws are put in place to protect the resource and ensure it will be around for many generations. Poachers on the other hand do not care about the future of wildlife or conservation. They are selfish and take from this world with no thought of tomorrow.

The difference can be seen in how hunters react to this poaching incident. Nobody is tougher on poachers than hunters. Hunters were calling for much stricter sentencing than the judge handed down. Every hunter I saw wanted more jail time, higher fines, and a lifetime hunting ban. This is exactly how hunters should act when confronted with bad actors. Poachers should not be tolerated in the hunting community.

Just like everything else in life, hunters need to remain balanced. We need to keep our motivations in check and not let them slip. It is more important than ever to be cognizant of our actions. Everything we do is being watched. Most importantly, we need to police ourselves and our hunting buddies. The future of hunting depends on showing the non-hunting world that we are relevant and a necessary part of the future of wildlife.

Chapter 9

Hunting Is Fun

Let us face it; no one ever has a hobby that they do not enjoy. Sure, some parts of a hobby are not always pleasant, but the overall feeling needs to be enjoyment or else people would not do it. In my experience, most people do not spend their weekends and other time off doing the same thing they do at work. Leisure time is for fun and enjoyment.

There might be few lucky people that enjoy their job, but for the vast majority of people, it is a means to an end. They do what they have to do to meet their responsibilities and to be able to afford what they enjoy doing. The 1980's song, " Working for the Weekend", could have been my grandpa's theme song except he did not like rock music. He worked to pay for his hunting passion.

The Navy drafted my grandpa during the Korean War. He became a boiler tender on a destroyer. After he got out, he could have made really good money with the skills the Navy taught him. His only apprehension was the working hours. He did not want to work weekends and be limited to just a few weeks of vacation a year, which was not enough to quench his hunting passion. So, the excellent paying job took a back seat.

He decided to find a job where he could work to meet his responsibilities, and the rigid schedule of an employer would not hamper his time to hunt. So, he started his own business with his dad and brother. They did roofing, siding, and general carpentry work. It was the perfect job. He would work super hard spring, summer, and early fall, but when deer season kicked off, he was in the woods hunting. Work hard, play hard was his mantra.

He found a way to pursue his passion, and he enjoyed it. He sacrificed money and other things to get enjoyment out of life. The good-paying job was just the latest in a long line of things that took a back seat to hunting. He dropped out of high school to hunt and fish more. He quit playing football because practice and games were during hunting season.

The only things that did not come between him and hunting were his family and his belief in God. As much as he loved hunting, he never hunted on Sunday. It was reasonably easy in the beginning since the blue laws were in effect, but even when they started allowing Sunday hunting in Ohio, he still went to church. My grandpa planned a large part of his life around hunting. It determined his career, played a significant role in his marriage, and how he raised his kids. He did all of that because hunting is fun.

The reason hunting is fun is because of the five motivations we have just mentioned. All of them bring to the table deep enjoyment and satisfaction. When you combine them, they are almost irresistible. Every hunt is made up of most, if not all, of the motivations. The challenge and adventure are always there in different degrees, and just being outside brings the spiritual connection. The camaraderie exists when you are with someone or when you are telling others about the hunt. And the meat is, well, I guess that only comes with a successful hunt.

I will be the first to admit that not every aspect of the hunt is fun. Sitting out in the cold for hours at a time until your feet are frozen, or the work of dragging a dead deer a mile in rough terrain, up hills, and over logs until your arms and legs burn and you feel like you cannot take another step. Trust me, none of that is fun at the time.

Fun at the time and fun looking back are entirely different things. When we look back, the pain and discomfort seem to fade away, and the satisfaction of a completed mission or even shared hardship becomes fun. The memory becomes pleasurable. I think it is because we overcame something and bettered ourselves.

It reminds me of exercising. There are times that you workout until you want to throw up. Your muscles burn, and you feel like crap. But once you complete the workout and you get all cleaned up, you start to feel pretty good. A good morning workout can set you up for positivity the rest of the day, even though it is not fun at the time. Looking back at past hunts, I cannot recall a hunt that was not fun. Some may not be as memorable as others, but I cannot think of one where I did not in some way enjoy myself.

One of my more memorable and most fun hunts was when I killed my first deer. I was 11 years old and hunting in West Virginia at my grandpa's cabin. It was Thanksgiving week, and it had been tough hunting. The first three days no one in our hunting party had even seen a buck, let alone put one on the ground. Now it is Thanksgiving morning, and my grandpa is taking me out to one of his favorite stands. We get in his truck and drive out to the spot. We park the truck, and he starts to get our gear ready when he realizes he left his rifle shells back at the house. So back in the truck we go and head back to the cabin.

He leaves me sitting in the truck to go inside and grab his ammo. When He comes back, he says, "I know we were planning on going to the Big Low Gap, but I have a feeling. We should go to the Old Field this morning." So, off we went.

Before I go on, let me tell you about the Old Field. It is not a field at all. It is a beautiful hardwood forest with lots of oak and poplars. The reason it is called the Old Field is that it was a field when my grandpa was a boy. He was in his sixties then, and it had not been a field for a good thirty to forty years. My brother and I always joke about it. I guess once you give a place a name, it sticks.

Anyway, the Old Field is where I sat opening morning of that week and saw fourteen does. It was an excellent spot but was a longer drive in the truck. The sun was already coming up when we got there, and it was pretty much daylight when we got to the stand. We sat for a few hours until my grandpa got restless. He told me to stay put, and he was going on a little walk. He planned to quietly push through a few bedding areas and hopefully jump a buck over to me.

He had been gone for about an hour when up from the bottom came a buck. He was cruising up the ridgeline about 120 yards out. I got my gun up, an old 6mm; took a rest on the tree stand rail and when he hit an opening, I shot. He took off up the hill ran for about 40 yards and stopped. He looked around like he was trying to figure out what to do next. That hesitation was all it took.

I aimed again and squeezed the trigger. BANG! He took off, up and over the hill. I did not know what happened. I did not know if I hit or I missed. But trust me, the adrenaline was running. My grandpa was just over the hill when I shot, so he came back to check on me. He said I was jumping all over the stand like a monkey. I was trying to tell him what happened, where the deer was, where it went, and I was not sure if I hit it all in one breath. He had no idea what I was saying.

He told me to settle down and stay in the stand and direct him to the place I last shot at the deer. I gave him directions, and before long, he gave me a hoot and motioned for me to come to him. He was standing next to some leaves that were covered in blood. He told me to follow the blood trail, and he was going to circle out in front.

I followed the blood up and over the hill. I was concentrating on the drops so carefully that when my grandpa fired a shot with his .30-06, I about peed myself. Right after that, my grandpa hooted. I knew that was a signal to come to him. When I got up next to him, he pointed and said, "What is laying right over there?" I looked to where he was pointing and could see a gray shape with the brown curl of the antlers sticking up from the ground. I was excited. I ran over to my buck and lifted its head and counted 8 points.

Anyone that has been hunting long knows that this is when the work begins. Killing the deer was the simple part. Now getting it back to the truck was going to be a job because the hill he ran over was, of course, in the opposite direction of where we parked. I was an eleven-year-old twerp and maybe weighed 100 lbs. soaking wet. This deer weighed about as much as I did. Good thing my grandpa was a strong man because I was not much help. I ended up carrying the rifles while he dragged the deer.

As we were dragging the deer up this old logging road next to this creek, and along came a deer. It walked within 25 yards of us. Good thing it was a doe because if it were a buck, my grandpa would have shot it, and we would be sitting here with two deer and still two miles from the truck. That deer did not even care that we were there. It slowly moved down the creek without a care in the world.

We finally got back to the truck and headed back to the cabin. As we turned down the driveway, my grandpa just laid on the horn. Everyone from the cabin came out, it had been a long week, and they knew we had something. My uncle dropped the tailgate so everyone could see my deer. At first, they thought my grandpa had got it, but when he said that it was mine everyone erupted into congratulations.

Everyone went out for the evening hunt except for my grandpa and me. We drove to town and checked in my deer and got ice cream - which is a kind of weird family tradition; if you kill a deer, you have to buy ice cream. After we got back to the cabin, we skinned him out and cut off the backstraps to go with the turkey my great-grandma was making for Thanksgiving dinner.

As we sat down that evening, I sat at the head of the table and led everyone in a Thanksgiving prayer. I had a lot to be thankful for that day. I had not only killed my first deer, but I had provided my family with meat. I also knew this was the first step of a long journey of deer hunting. I will forever remember that day. It ranks up there with my wedding and the birth of my children; it was a rite of passage. That day I became a provider, and in my eyes, became a man. Even though I still had a lot of growing up to do, this was an important milestone.

That hunt and many like it was fun. I enjoyed every moment of it. It also incorporated every motivation that we have mentioned. The meat is pretty obvious. We ate that for dinner. The camaraderie was being with my grandpa and telling the story to the rest of the hunters. The entire hunt was an adventure that had many challenges along the way. And the whole experience was deeply spiritual.

Hunting is fun. What motivates us to go hunting is the reason it is fun. It is a challenging adventure filled with camaraderie and rewarded with spiritual fulfillment and hopefully, in the end, delicious meat to share with friends and family.

Chapter 10

Conservation

While completing my history degree in college, one of my projects was to do a 20-page report on any aspect of Ohio history. The topic I chose was, of all things, the history of deer hunting in the State. Before I started, the only thing I knew was that whitetail deer were extirpated from the state sometime around the turn of the 20th century. Ohio now boasts one of the healthiest deer populations in the country.

The premise of my report was how did we get from nothing to abundance. It was not a super complicated story, but it was an eye-opening one. In the early 1930s, the state started with approximately 30 deer that they imported from out of state. They put them in an enclosure in southern Ohio so that they could get used to the new environment and then the following year they took down the fence.

The deer began to spread. By the 1950s, Ohio had its first deer season in three counties. At first, the bag limit was one buck, and there was not a very high success rate during the early years. Slowly, as populations spread northward, more counties were opened to hunting. Every year deer populations increased until they hit their peak in the 1990s.

Today, deer thrive across the state, and it has become a premier destination for hunters from all across the country. Deer hunting is a large business in Ohio; it brings in millions of dollars annually to local economies all around the state. Who do we have to thank for the fantastic deer populations and the economic growth that came with them? Hunters. It was a hunting club that banded together and raised money for the initial project. They built the enclosure and helped set up the game management plan that brought us to where we are today.

Their desire to hunt motivated their conservation activities. They wanted more robust game populations that would lead to their success in the field. Some people may say that this is selfish, but in the long run, we see that what they did benefited us all.

There are stories like this all across the country. Animal populations have been brought back from near extinction, to flourishing. In the past 100 years, North America is experiencing a renaissance of wildlife. Pronghorn, bison, wolves, eagles, and grizzly bears are just a few examples of recovered species.

Perhaps the most amazing recovery has been the wild turkey. The not so majestic bird that Benjamin Franklin lobbied to make our national bird was in serious trouble at the turn of the century. But through hunting organizations like the Wild Turkey Federation, their numbers have exploded.

The process took a while to get going and was full of trial and error, but once they figured out how to reintroduce the birds successfully, things took off. The breakthrough came when they realized that they could not raise wild turkey on farms and release them into the wild. They needed to transplant wild birds from healthy populations.

The cannon capture net is just a cool as it sounds. They would bait an area that turkeys frequented with corn or some other grain. When the entire flock was in the capture zone, someone in a blind would hit a button and fire a net over the turkeys. The turkeys would be collected and transported to a new environment that had no turkeys. This process was repeated many times over. Wild turkeys now occupy more places today than at any other time in history. Their populations are thriving, and we have hunters to thank.

Hunters often point to conservation as a reason for why they hunt, but you will notice I did not list conservation as a hunting motivation. The reason is because I believe conservation is a byproduct or benefit of hunting. Conservation is motivated by hunting, and a reason not to go hunting.

The difference between motivation and benefit can be complicated. A motive is what propels us to do something, while a benefit is an outcome. I will admit there is some overlap. All of the motivations offer direct benefits, but there are some benefits that are not necessarily motivations. Conservation is probably the best example of this. There are very few hunters that get up at three a.m. and drive three hours to sit in minus 3-degree weather with conservation on their mind. However, all of the five motivations I mentioned can and are reasons you do things like that.

Now I do not want you to think I am down-playing how hunters feel about conservation. Hunters know this is extremely vital to the future of hunting. So much so that hunters are willing to tax themselves and are willing to pay ever-increasing license fees to advance it.

It is a reciprocal endeavor. Hunting pays for conservation, and conservation makes hunting better, just like the hunt club that brought deer back to Ohio. Their motivation for conservation was, in a way, self-serving. We have the same motivation. All hunters desire to be more successful, and they do what they can to improve their chances. Conservation improves those chances. At least that is how most hunters take their first step into the world of conservation.

I did not start hunting waterfowl until I was an adult — a big part of the reason why was because I had no one to teach me. No one in my family

63

hunted ducks and geese, and I did not know where or how to begin. That was until I met a guy at church named Zach. He was an avid waterfowler and agreed to take me along.

We rented a blind in a state park; threw out decoys and waited. We saw hundreds of birds, but they all stayed out of range. We never got a shot that day, but I was hooked. The whole experience of sitting in a blind, spotting birds, calling, and just spending time with good people was terrific. It was different from deer hunting where you have to wait until you get back from sitting in the stand to talk about the hunt.

To make a long story short, I fell in love with duck hunting and waterfowl in general. And to celebrate my new-found love, I joined Ducks Unlimited. The reason I joined was that I wanted to be more successful, meet more waterfowl hunters, and give back. It was the first conservation club I joined. As you can see, it was hunting that brought me to conservation, not the other way around.

The same goes for game management, which is a subcategory of conservation. It is a byproduct and a tool of hunting, not a motivation. No one goes out hunting to control populations exclusively. Even when it comes to predator hunting, they go out because of their mix of the five motivations, though the benefit of population control is in the front of their mind.

I will take a deeper dive into predator hunting in a later chapter, because even though the motivations are the same, they are a little more nuanced when compared to hunting animals that we typically eat, and I think it deserves a complete explanation.

Hunters see themselves as stewards of nature and managing game populations is one of those responsibilities. Hunters work hand in glove with state wildlife agencies to keep wildlife populations stable. This cooperation is a huge benefit for the agencies.

Hunting is a huge cost saver in wildlife management. Hunters pay to hunt. Wildlife management costs money in areas that forbid hunting. Agencies spend hundreds of thousands of dollars a year, controlling non-huntable populations, which include controlling deer populations in urban centers and populations of protected animals.

A great example of how this works can be seen when hunting is eliminated as a tool for wildlife managers. Back in the 1990's, mountain lion hunting was banned in California, even though there was no scientific reason for doing so. Their populations were stable and not even close to being endangered. Nevertheless, the ban passed on a ballot measure based on emotion.

Now California is forced to manage mountain lion populations by paying trappers and hunters to do something they would have gladly paid money. The interesting thing is that the paid trappers and hunters kill just about the same amount of lions that hunters would have killed if hunting them was still permitted.

What the ban caused was the waste of hides and meat because it became the property of the state. None of it could be kept by the paid hunters because the lions were protected animals. The ban is doing more harm than good and encourages the waste of a resource that would otherwise be utilized. The waste is appalling, but reinstituting lion hunting could fix it. The killed lions could be used for their hide and meat, but it would also be a revenue stream — instead of expenditure for California's wildlife agency.

Hunters are the world's true conservationists. Some environmentalist and anti-hunting groups have hijacked that term and have tried to pass off preservation as conservation. Preservation means no use, while conservation means wise use. When someone tells you to conserve water, they are not telling you to stop using water. They want you to use that resource wisely, so there is enough for everyone now, as well as for future generations. It is the same way in wildlife and habitat conservation. Hunters seek to use the resources in such a way that it is available for future generations to use and enjoy.

While conservation is not a direct motivator, it is a benefit and one of the main reasons that hunting remains necessary in a modern world. Hunting gives value to animals and habitat. I will take a deep dive into this concept when I talk about trophy hunting in a following chapter.

Hunters want more elk on the mountain and deer in the field. They also want more wild places to hunt and want those places teeming with game and nongame species. We want clean water and clean air. Hunting has brought us to be conservation-minded for the benefit of all wildlife and humanity.

Chapter 11

Respect for other Motives

A few years back, my sister killed her first buck. It was by no means a monster, just a little fork horn, but she was proud of it. So proud of it that she got the deer mounted and is now hanging in her living room. What is also pretty cool is that my brother got it on film. You can watch her put a beautiful 20-yard shot with a crossbow right through the boilermaker. You could hear the excitement in her voice after the shot. There is absolutely no doubt that she was happy and excited.

We uploaded the video to social media, and for the most part, it received positive results, but there were a few commenters that decided to act negatively. Two stood out. One guy said, "Should have let it grow" and another was upset that she used a crossbow. Both of the comments bothered me for the same reason. They decided to use their motives as a standard to judge my sister. In other words, if you do not hunt like me and follow the same set of criteria I choose, then you are wrong. This type of logic is seriously flawed, and when you look at the particulars, it becomes almost absurd.

Let us take the first comment, "You should have let it grow." First of all, the commenter lives in Oklahoma and we live in Ohio. I am still scratching my head to figure out why he cares. There is absolutely no way he would ever have a chance at killing that deer. Maybe he is so concerned that my sister was short-changed with killing that buck, and if she only waited until it had bigger antlers, she could have a better experience. Who knows what he was thinking. I cannot think of a rational argument as to why a hunter would look down on other hunters' kill. As long as they followed all of the laws, there should be no issue.

The other comment I mentioned pertained to the use of a crossbow. Once again, who cares? She followed the law. It was a legal weapon. I like crossbows. I have killed deer with a rifle, shotgun, muzzleloader, compound bow, and a crossbow. I enjoyed all of them. What I like about the crossbow is probably the reason a lot of hunters hate it. It is easy. The ease of use does two things. It breaks down barriers of entry for new hunters and adds years to older hunters. I know young kids who use crossbows, my grandma uses a crossbow, and guess what, so do many hunters in between.

I think the resistance to crossbows comes from hunters who believe that just because they restrict themselves by using a harder weapon, that means others must follow those same restrictions. My cousin shoots a recurve and he is voluntarily making it harder on himself to kill deer. Because he chose that challenge, does that mean other hunters should not hunt with a compound? That is absurd.

Hunters get into arguments about all sorts of things. Sometimes these arguments can become downright nasty. One of the worst cases I have seen was a couple of hunters talking about Antler Point Restrictions (APR's). One was adamantly for and the other against them. Neither one was listening to the other, and neither one wanted to budge.

APR's are when a game department restrict what bucks can be killed based on its antlers. For example, in Pennsylvania, you can only kill a buck that has an antler with at least 3 points on one side. Only a few states have implemented rules like this, but other states have kicked around the idea, and that's when the arguments start.

APR's are probably one of the best examples of conflicting motivations there is. It pits two types of hunters against each other, the meat-minded hunter versus the challenge-minded hunter. The proposal is usually brought up by the challenge-minded hunter. His goal is to have more mature and bigger bucks to hunt, so he wants the government to implement rules that favor his motivations. This perceived attack makes the meat hunter mad. He wants to shoot the first buck to walk by, fill the freezer, and call it a day.

Which one is right? Personally, I fall on the side of the meat hunter, but I do understand the hunter's point of view. In my opinion, the least amount of restriction is best. If you show me a situation that shows that certain regulations are better for deer and hunting as a whole I will defiantly support it. However, if your goal is to amplify your motivations at the expense of others then I will resist you every time.

All hunters are different, and we do not always know what motivates them. Even for myself, my motivations have changed from year to year. Back in 2015, I shot one of the smallest does I have ever killed. I know a lot of hunters that would have let it walk, but I did not, and I had an understandable reason. I wanted deer meat. I had just gotten back from a military deployment and faced an empty freezer, plus I had only a few days to hunt until the season closed. I was in an, "if it's brown, it's down" mode. The first deer to walk by was going home with me. And this small doe decided to step out from the woods behind the house while we were eating lunch. I have absolutely zero regrets about shooting that deer. My motivation was 100% meat. I was happy to have that deer and did not care who disagreed with me.

The next year things were different. I was not in a time crunch. I killed a nice doe early in the season, and I waited on a nice buck. The buck I was after never showed up, so I shot another doe at the end of the season. I passed up at least a half dozen small bucks that year. They were not the deer I was after.

You can see how my motivations shifted over a year. In my case, it was all based on circumstances. One year I was deployed overseas and lacked time in the woods; the other I had all season to hunt. Neither of my motivations was wrong; they were just different. And if they can be different from year to year, think of how different they can be from hunter to hunter.

We all hunt for different reasons. We all have a unique mix of the five motivations which shapes our hunting decisions. Your reasons are not my reasons, and honestly, unless you are breaking the law or being unethical, there is no good reason to judge another hunter's kill, choice of weapon, management style, or any other crazy idea you can think up. We are all on the same team. We are all hunters that share a common love for the outdoors and enjoy the pursuit. We are all in this together.

Chapter 12

Predator Hunting

Coyotes are a reasonably new phenomenon east of the Mississippi. I had never seen one in Ohio until the early 2000s. I knew they were there. I had seen tracks, and I occasionally heard them howling at night, but had never laid eyes on one.

The first coyote I have ever seen happened when I was sitting on a tree line overlooking a field with my .243, hunting groundhogs. Out of nowhere, two animals started running across the field about 150 yards away. My first thought was deer, but that quickly disappeared when one of them stopped. "That's a coyote," I said to myself, and I drew down.

I squeezed the trigger, and it dropped. I walked over to it and saw it was a large female. I had shot her right through the neck, not my best shot, but it did the job. I was excited. This encounter was a first for me, and for anyone who hunted, with us for that matter. Many more coyote encounters would come over the next few years. Sightings would become more frequent, the tracks would increase, and you could hear them almost every night. They are established and not going anywhere. Not just on our property, but all across the nation, coyotes have become targets of opportunity. It does not matter what kind of hunt you are on; when you see a coyote, it turns into a coyote hunt.

That is what happened this past turkey season. I was sitting in a clearing first thing in the morning. I had not hit my call when a coyote bounded out across from me and came across the clearing. I swung my shotgun across and dropped her with one shot to the head at 20 yards. Like I said, every hunt turns into a coyote hunt when they show up.

Coyotes occupy a unique place in the hunting landscape, especially on the East Coast that has only recently become part of their range. They are looked at with contempt by some and as competition by others. They are incredibly adaptable and can thrive just about anywhere.

Coyote hunting is probably the least controversial type of predator hunting. I believe it is because coyotes have adapted so well to the modern environment. They are not only affecting rural populations, but also have had an adverse effect in urban areas. Every day people's pets disappear into the jaws of a coyote never to be seen again. That is what happened to one of my friend's Jack Russel Terriers. She had let him out into the backyard like normal, and it was not too long after that that a coyote slipped in and carried him away.

Stories like this are commonplace across the country, and I have heard of these incidents happening in my small town. Now when anyone sees a coyote, they quickly post it in our town's Facebook group, warning people to keep an eye on their pets. For most people, me shooting a coyote is not controversial. But switch coyote for a more charismatic animal, like a wolf, bear, or mountain lion, and then you start to receive pushback. However, the same principles related to management apply to them as well. I believe this is for a couple of reasons.

First, most people are not directly affected by these predators. These animals have not adapted as well to the urban environment as coyotes. They do not eat as many pets, and for the most part, stay away from humans. Some of this is changing, however. Black bears are becoming more of a nuisance, and mountain lions are starting to make appearances in more urban settings, especially in

California. But for the most part, people are not worried about them.

Second, bears and wolves occupy a unique niche in our culture. We grew up with teddy bears and images of the majestic wolf. Their true nature has been tempered by culture in a way that has stripped them of their brutality. In a way, they have ceased to be predators and have become cultural icons.

These reasons make predator hunting a hot button issue for a lot of non-hunters. They do not understand management strategies or understand the motives of why people kill them. I mentioned before that hunting for meat is the easiest motivation for non-hunters to follow. They understand why we hunt deer, elk, moose, or any other animal that seems to have a domestic counterpart. Non-hunters know it is for meat and for the most part, accept hunting as a way to acquire it.

Predators have no domestic counterpart, so they are not typically thought of as hunted for meat. Even though many hunters eat bear and mountain lion, the negative image persists, and the approval for hunting drops. But food is one of the reasons we do hunt them, just not directly. We hunt them because we are in competition with them for food. Their food is our food.

In the United States and Canada, wild game is a huge food source. Hunters kill approximately six million deer each hunting season, and each deer can provide anywhere from 40-100 pounds of meat. Conservatively, that works out to 240 million pounds of meat, and that's just deer. We have yet to add in elk, moose, caribou, waterfowl, and other small game. So the true number is much higher.

In other words, we have a massive renewable food resource that we need to protect. Like I mentioned before, we compete with predators. Now, this does not mean that we plan on or want to wipe these animals off the landscape. Hunters understand that all creatures have a place in this world and it would be an egregious sin to hunt any creature to extinction purposely. That being said, predators need to be managed.

To understand why they need management, let us talk a little bit about predator and prey relationships. Back in the 1920's, there was an excellent study on the connection between rabbits and foxes. They found that as the rabbit population multiplied, they provided a food source for the foxes, which resulted in more foxes. When the increased number of foxes ate the rabbits, the food supply disappeared, which led to the foxes dying off. When the fox population dropped, the rabbit population rebounded, creating a new food supply for the foxes. It is a self-perpetuating cycle

This same cycle can be applied to other predator/prey relationships, for instance, wolves/ elk and moose/bear. The rabbit/fox cycle takes about ten years to complete, which is surprisingly fast because rabbits breed like rabbits, and they can recover relatively quickly. Quick recovery is not true for the other animals mentioned. Elk and moose have one to two offspring a year; the cycle takes a long time to run its course.

I know what some of you are thinking, it is a natural cycle, and we should just let it play out. The problem with that is the millions of pounds of game meat that people use for food. That need is not going anywhere when game populations are in the extreme down part of the cycle, which could last for a decade or more. In the absence of wild game to eat, people will turn to domestically produced meat. Cattle operations will have to grow, which leads to the clearing of more land, which means less habitat for wild animals.

To protect a valuable food resource and protect habitat, predators need to be managed. What wildlife managers are trying to achieve is a steady population of both game animals and predators. They strive to keep game animals at populations that can both sustain human harvest and provide food the predators.

Predator populations can only be kept in check by hunters and trappers. A certain number of predators must be taken out of the ecosystem every year so that the balance can be maintained. Wild food is a resource, and we must make sure that it remains sustainable.

As you can see, food is an essential aspect of predator hunting. That is why I shoot coyotes when I see them. With every coyote, I kill, I give a few more deer, rabbits, and other small game animals a chance to survive. Which, in turn, I can hunt and provide my family with food.

I understand that it is hard for people to get over the cultural attachment to these iconic animals. Trying to explain wildlife management in 140 characters is nearly impossible. Wildlife management is complicated. There are many moving parts and interconnections that are not always apparent, but the system we have put together here in North America works.

The system is known to most sportsmen and conservationist as the "North American Hunting Model." It is a system that was set up at the beginning of the 20th century to deal with the disappearance of game and other animals.

When Europeans arrived in North America, wildlife was abundant. Millions of bison roamed the Great Plains, and there was a beaver in every stream. To people of that day, it looked like an inexhaustible resource, a resource of food and fur that would never run out.

Settlers who looked at the land also shared this view. They saw the forests as inexhaustible sources of timber and the land beneath them valuable for farming. Millions of acres of wildlife habitat were cleared to make room for progress. As a result, overhunting and habitat destruction decimated wildlife population all across the continent. Some animals, like the passenger pigeon and the eastern bison, were actually driven to extinction. Other animals like the whitetail deer, that seem so familiar today, were extirpated from much of their natural range. At the turn of the century, wildlife was in dire straits.

The reason people can see deer and other wildlife in their backyards today is because of hunters. Hunters and anglers led the charge to bring about the changes needed to stop the decimation of wildlife and started setting the groundwork for the modern wildlife management system we use today.

Over the last one hundred years, wildlife population has rebounded to almost unbelievable levels. Deer in states such as Ohio went from a population of zero in the year 1900 to over 650,000 in 2015. Hunters reestablished wild turkeys to all of their native range. They now even exist in places that never held turkeys.

There are now huntable populations of elk in five states east of the Mississippi. Wolves have been reintroduced to western states and are thriving. Grizzly bears are ready to come off of the endangered species list. And this is just a sampling of what has been accomplished by sportsmen.

Everyone has benefited from what hunters have done. Hikers, kayakers, and campers reap the benefits of the wild places that modern-day sportsmen have worked for and paid to preserve. So, when you look out your back door and see a wild world, thank a hunter because it did not happen by accident.

I support the North American Hunting Model of Conservation because it works, and if a system works, it does not need fixing. Science supports the system, and the results are irrefutable. The model includes predator management, which is an integral part of the system. It has helped sustain a healthy balance of predator and prey animals that ensure sustainable harvest of meat for humans.

Predator hunting is one of the hardest types of hunting to get the non-hunting public to understand. But if you stick to the science and show how all wildlife benefits, it can be done.

Chapter 13

Trophy Hunting

When I was five years old, my grandpa told me he was going to take me squirrel hunting the following day. I was super excited to go; I barely slept that night. In the morning, we got up early and drove down to a property he had permission to hunt. We headed out into the woods and sat by an old oak tree and waited for the world to wake up.

Now remember I am five and this is only the second time I had ever gone squirrel hunting, so spotting squirrels with leaves still on the trees was extremely difficult for me. My grandpa probably spotted half a dozen squirrels, but my untrained eye could not locate them.

Also, it was hard for me to keep still, so staying in one spot was not an option. After an hour at one place, he decided to take me walking around. We would walk for a bit then find a tree to sit by for at most half an hour, then I would get fidgety and we would have to move.

On one of our little excursions, we found something I had never seen in the woods, and even still, I have not seen it again. We found a baby squirrel that had fallen out of the nest and was lying shivering on the ground. My grandpa picked it up, and he was still alive. He tucked it in his shirt to warm it up, and before long, he started to become more active. The baby squirrel began doing laps around my grandpa's waist. He got him out, and we fed the little guy a granola bar, and when he finally fell asleep, we tucked him back into my grandpa's shirt and continued the hunt.

We walked a bit farther when my grandpa spotted a "big ol' fox squirrel" up in a hickory tree.

He got me ready and helped me steady the gun. I do not know how long it took, but I eventually got the crosshairs on the squirrel and prepared to squeeze the trigger.

Now before I tell you what happened next, I want to tell you about the gun I was using. Remember I am five and even though I had shot before, I had never shot a gun with open sites. All I had shot were rifles with scopes, so my grandpa felt and was probably right that if I were going to kill a squirrel, I would need to use a scope. He set me up with a 20-gauge shotgun that had a mounted scope for my grandma. I had never shot this gun before, and now when I look back, I am pretty sure that was on purpose. He did not want me to know how much it kicked and felt I would have a better chance of getting a squirrel if I was not expecting it.

So now, back to the hunt. I squeezed the trigger and boom. What happened next is a blur. The scope came back and knocked me right above the eye, giving me a nasty cut. The squirrel dropped from the tree, and my grandpa took off after it to make sure it did not get away. I remember blood rolling down my face and looking at my grandpa who was smiling while he had his foot on my squirrel. He finally realized what had happened and came over to me. He ripped his undershirt and made a makeshift bandage and got the bleeding to stop. I picked up my squirrel, and we headed back to the truck.

Since then, I have shot so many squirrels I have lost count, but that hunt will always be the most memorable. I shot my first squirrel, got a baby squirrel (who I named Buster) for a pet, and a scar to remember it all. But that was not the only thing I had to remember it. A few months later, I went over to my grandpa's house, and he had a surprise for me. He had taken my squirrel to my uncle, who is a taxidermist and had it mounted. That squirrel has been with me for over 30 years. It is more to me than just a dead animal on the wall. It is the memory of that hunt and all the subsequent adventures I have gone on with my grandpa. It has become more than just a squirrel.

That is what I believe is the biggest misconception about trophy hunting. Many people see it as just a head on a wall put up there for bragging rights. They think people get mounts done to show off to others; while there may be a little truth to that, it is by no means the complete picture.

I have a handful of mounts and skulls displayed around my house. They are there more for me than for others. Just like the squirrel, every mount tells a story and is a memorial to that animal and the hunt. Not a day goes by that I don't walk by them and am reminded of the good times, hardships, and adventure that they represent.

I would be lying if I said I do not enjoy showing them off and having people impressed by them. The largest buck I have ever shot hangs in a prominent place in my living room, and when visitors come to the house, they cannot miss it. Even those who are not super familiar with hunting recognize it as an exceptional buck, and it receives a lot of compliments, and those compliments stroke my ego.

But that deer is contrasted by what is hanging next to it, the fan from my first turkey. It is not an impressive bird. The fan is small and the three and a half-inch beard is not remarkable. The mount has a place to display the spurs, but on such a young bird, they were nonexistent, so I left them off. I do not think I have ever received a compliment about the turkey, but it hangs there in prominence because of all the hard work I put into hunting it.

This is the reason why a majority of hunters get mounts. It memorializes the hunt and shows off the accomplishment as well as showcases the animal.

They are not purely done for ego and bragging rights. The term "trophy hunter" has become a loaded term in the past few decades. People see the heads on the wall and assume they know the whole story behind them. This flawed thinking has become especially true for animals killed in Africa.

Everyone has heard of Cecil the Lion. When a hunter killed him, it made global headlines, and all hell broke loose. The hunter who killed him started receiving death threats, and he even had to close his business. His life will never be the same. I cannot vouch for what his motives were. I have never met the man and cannot judge his character. But the entire incident got me to take an in-depth look at what is trophy hunting in Africa and if people were being unfair to the hunter.

I already had extensive knowledge of the North American Hunting Model, but only a rudimentary understanding of the African Hunting Model. I was forced to do some studying and some deep thinking to explain what it is, how it works, and why I believe trophy hunting is necessary for wildlife conservation in Africa.

Right now, the biggest issue facing African wildlife is habitat loss. We have this same issue in North America, but for socio-economic reasons, this problem is magnified in Africa. Africa is full of developing countries that are trying to pull themselves out of poverty. This struggle means the development of once wild spaces.

Every piece of land that does not have an economic value must be transformed into land that does. The rainforests of Ivory Coast are providing no commercial value as rainforests, so they are being burned down so farmers can plant cocoa and other commodities. Also, grasslands in the sub-Saharan are being plowed up, irrigated, and crops are being planted.

Not only does this remove wildlife habitat, but it also sets up human-wildlife conflicts. The animals that still live there now see the newly developed agriculture as a new food source. The farmers are now in competition with the animals for the crops. To them, these animals have zero value. They see these animals as having a negative value and their existence is a direct threat to their livelihoods.

This issue is where trophy hunting comes in. It gives value to animals. What once was a liability, has now become an asset. It is easier to tolerate an animal that eats up a few hundred dollars worth of crops if you can get a hunter to pay you a few thousand dollars to hunt it. The same concept also works with habitat. It gives people a reason to keep wild places wild. If you have a tract of land and you want it to make you money, usually this would mean having to develop it. But with trophy hunting, you can leave it be and manage the wildlife on it for a profit. Trophy hunting has preserved countless acres using this process.

Also, just like North America, managing populations is essential. One of the best examples is breaking down why the hunting of the iconic elephant is so crucial. Killing them is hugely controversial, but necessary. Elephant populations are indeed declining but hunting them is still very important to ensure their survival. I know it seems counterproductive to save an animal by killing them, but there is a reason.

The reason goes back to what I mentioned earlier. Habitat destruction is the greatest threat to African animals. Because of the habitat destruction, elephants can no longer migrate the same way they did in the past. The development has restricted these animals to smaller chunks of suitable habitat. These smaller chunks of habitat can only sustain a certain number of elephants. If the elephant populations get too large for that specific piece of

83

land, they overeat that habitat making it able to sustain fewer elephants. In time past the elephants would move on, but now they have nowhere else to go.

If left unmanaged, they will eventually eat themselves into a habitat cycle that would support far fewer elephants than an elephant herd managed by hunting. Just like the fox-rabbit cycle, laid out in the last chapter. This same thing would happen with elephants and their habitat. Elephants would eat their habitat to the point where the land could not support them. The elephants would subsequently starve, allowing vegetation to recover, which would enable elephants to start recovering and restart the cycle.

This scenario is the best-case scenario if the populations are left unmanaged. What could happen is that the unmanaged population could damage the habitat to such an extent that it never recovers and we are eventually left with no elephants.

Elephant hunting is strictly regulated. Only excess elephants are allowed to be taken by hunters. Excess elephants are usually males and females past breeding age, but some young males are also taken. By selectively taking only individual members of a population, it keeps the population at roughly the same size. This management style creates a balance of habitat and animals that is sustainable.

As can be seen, the shooting of some elephants is necessary for preserving the habitat and sustainability of the herd. Now comes the question of how best to perform these essential killings. The obvious answer is regulated hunting. It is the same thing we do in North America. The only difference is who is making the kill.

In North America, we rely on local hunters to control wildlife populations. In Africa, they rely on foreign hunters to do the same thing. The reason is simple economics. Local Africans cannot pay as much as foreigners. Many have trouble just getting by, let alone having the resources to participate in regulated hunting. The rates are high because they have to be able to offset the cost of not developing habitat and keeping locals tolerant of animal interactions.

Foreign hunters can pay these necessary high fees. And they are happy to do so. They are motivated by four of the five motivations for hunting. The only one missing is meat. This reason is where I believe a lot of people take issues with the foreign hunters and the term trophy hunter gets tarnished.

Meat is the most tangible of the motivations. It is easily understood and accepted. When you take that way, it becomes more abstract. Challenge, adventure, and spiritual fulfillment are hard to measure and are only apparent to the individual doing the hunting. The only tangible thing left for them to see is the trophy on the wall. The meat is not entirely gone from the equation however; nothing is wasted. All the meat from these hunts goes to feed the local populations. It is just that the person who pulls the trigger does not eat the meat.

As you can see, trophy hunting is not as cut and dry as anti-hunting organizations would want us to believe. It is complicated and hard to see how it all fits together. This is a basic overview of how it works and why it is necessary. I am not going to pretend that it is a perfect system. African hunting does have its issues with government corruption, canned hunts, and poaching. However, the system does work, and right now it is the only chance African wildlife has for survival.

Chapter 14

Why it Matters

Two deer seasons ago my then seven-year-old son was able to sit in the tree stand with me during the opening day of deer gun season here in Ohio. This hunt was not the first time he was able to sit with me, but it would become one of the most memorable. He had come with me bow hunting a few times, and I had taken him out squirrel hunting, but our success was limited to only a couple squirrels.

My son is still learning to sit still, and like most kids, he gets cold quick. Based on past experiences, I knew we would only get a couple of hours before he would want to head back to the house. I selected a stand that was reasonably easy to get to, so I could walk him back and then continue the hunt.

Lucky for us that little hike would not be needed. We had only been in the stand 20 minutes when a pair of bucks came off the neighbor's property and into the field we were watching. I gave them a quick glance with my binoculars and decided to take the big 8-point.

They crossed right in front of us at 80 yards, but I rushed the shot. I saw the snow fly up right underneath the buck. He turned to run, but it seemed that the deer did not know from where the shot had come, so he hesitated. That was all I needed. I shot a second, and he dropped his head and started slowly moving for cover. I knew I had hit him, but he was still on his feet, so I racked another shell into my 12-gauge, and sent another slug downrange. He lurched forward and made a beeline towards the trees with the hobble that indicated a high shoulder hit.

He barely made it into the tree line when he crashed. He kicked for a second then laid his head down. I looked over at my son, and he was shaking; he had buck fever. I looked back at the deer 50 yards away, and it lifted its head. One more shot rang out, and that was all she wrote.

We walked over to the deer, and what I thought was an 8-point was a 10-point. It was a mainframe eight with one split brow and a kicker coming off its right beam. My son does not show a lot of emotion, but I could tell he was excited. We grabbed the deer, drug him down the hill away from the stand, and I got to show him the finer points of field dressing. I showed him the heart, lungs and liver. I showed him where the three of my four shots went through. He asked a ton of questions that I answered as best as I could. We bonded over the gut pile. That was a hunt we both will never forget.

And that is why hunting matters. I want to be able to pass hunting along to my son and daughters, just like it was passed on to me by my grandpa. I spent countless weekends hunting and fishing with my grandpa. He taught me about nature and life. The times I spent hunting was some of the greatest memories I had growing up, and I am so happy that my children can join me in my passion, if they choose.

I try to imagine all the adventures we will have and not just the big things like them killing their first deer, but I look forward to all the little things. I remember my grandpa always having Werther's Original hard candy in the tree stand. He would feed me one piece after another to keep me quiet and sitting still. That is something that sticks with me to this day. Every deer season, I grab a bag of Werther's and keep it in my pack. It reminds me of hunting with him again. Now when my kids hunt with me, I pass that little tradition on to them.

Looking back, I see the good old days filled with memories and good times, but when I look forward, some things that I see scare me. The way things are going, I am not sure how much of my grandpa's heritage I will be able to pass down to not just my children, but also to my grandchildren.

Hunting has become controversial. It is under attack daily by anti-hunting groups that want to see it fall away in antiquity and become a remnant of the past. At any given time, there are dozens of anti-hunting bills being introduced to legislatures all over the country, seeking to ban little tiny pieces of our heritage. Some laws have already passed, and more are sure to be on the way.

As I see it, two main factors are leading us down this road. First, is the fact that we as a society are becoming disconnected from nature. People do not even know from where their food comes; there is a disconnect, they seem to forget that the package of meat they bought in the grocery store came from a living, breathing animal. It never even crosses most people's minds that something had to die for them to eat.

How wildlife is portrayed as a whole, also plays into this disconnect. Disney's talking animals have corrupted the last few generations. Bambi, Winnie the Pooh, and other characters have all influenced our culture, which believes that without man, nature would live in harmony.

This idea could not be farther from the truth. Nature is brutal and savage. While sitting in the tree stand one evening, I saw a red-tailed hawk destroy a morning dove. The dove was sitting on a branch when all of a sudden, there was an explosion of feathers. I saw the hawk fly away with the dove. He landed in a nearby tree and ripped the dove's guts out and feasted on them. It was one of the most savage scenes I have ever seen in person.

How the general public treats nature is evidence of this. I just watched a video of a young girl being flipped head over heels by a bison at Yellowstone, because her parents allowed her to get too close. They did not respect the power or wildness of that massive animal, and she paid the price. Thankfully she was treated for only minor injuries and will be fine. But still, the point remains wild animals are dangerous, and people underestimate them.

The second reason feeds on the ignorance of the first. News and information move faster now than at any other point in history. Couple that with outrage culture and that gives you a perfect storm to create outrage against hunting. Cecil the lion, is one example, but there are many others.

All it takes is killing an iconic animal by, a wealthy person, and the torches and pitchforks come out. It does not take much to set people off. Joe Rogan has mentioned this on his podcast more than once. He decided to try an experiment on his Instagram. He posted a series of photos starting with a dead fish; nobody cared. He posted a picture of some chicken meat; still, no one cared. Finally, he posted pictures of bear meat, not a dead bear just a package of meat labeled bear and received hate for it.

People's disconnect from nature makes them easy targets for the emotional arguments from anti-hunting groups. It does not matter how much money hunting raises for conservation or how much habitat preserved; the emotional case will always seem to win out.

But all is not lost, there is still hope for hunting's future, and it is up to hunters to ensure its survival. There are steps hunters can take to show the non-hunting public that hunting is a necessary part of life and that it still has a purpose in a modern world.

Hunters can turn the tide of negative press, but it is going to take effort. We can longer sit in our little groups and mind our own business. We need to reach out and be ambassadors for our sport and engage the public thoughtfully and respectfully. But before we can do this, we need to clean up our own house; there is too much division in the hunting community. We need to come together, and we can do that with understanding. The five motives I outlined in this book is the foundation of this understanding. They provide a way for you to decipher why another hunter does, what they do, and where you can find common ground. Because once we find common ground, the differences do not seem so big.

The next thing hunters need to do is arm themselves with knowledge. They need to understand why they hunt and why other people hunt. They need to have answers for some of the more difficult questions that are guaranteed to come up, like trophy hunting and the necessity of predator hunting. When Cecil the lion was killed, I had multiple people who knew I was a hunter come up to me and ask me, "Why did Cecil have to die?" I understood far less about hunting in Africa then I do now. I bumbled my ways through those conversations, and I think I made a positive impact, but knowing what I do now, I believe it could have gone so much better.

Also, we need to remember that we are teachers, and we need to have patience with the people we are trying to teach and to do our best to be respectful. Remember, you cannot start a conversation by calling someone an idiot and then expect them to hear you. I want you to think back to your school days and think of the most impactful teacher you ever had. Why were they impactful? What did they do to unlock your curiosity? Most importantly, what did they do that made you respect what they said? I am willing to guess they impacted your life because they were patient, respectful, and did not treat you like you were an idiot. Make them your model and go and do likewise.

I remember a conversation I had with a friend while I was in college that had recently decided to become a vegetarian. She became a vegetarian in response to how some animals are treated on some farms. She had little exposure to hunting and was curious about it. We talked for several hours about how hunting, if done right, is one of the most ethical ways to acquire meat. At the end of the conversation, she told me that hunting was not something she was interested in doing. However, she had no problem with me, or hunters like me, participating in it.

I consider that a win. That conversation could have gone the complete opposite direction if I was not somewhat knowledgeable about why I hunted and the basics of conservation. I was also respectful and patient and was able to walk my friend through in a way that made sense. She will probably never be a hunter, but she understands where we are coming from and is respectful of it.

It is these types of interactions that are the most important. Personal connections flow deeper than connections made online. I do not know of any person who changed their minds arguing on Facebook or Instagram, but I have had people with whom I have had a personal relationship alter their views.

We are the stewards of hunting and will be ultimately responsible if it fails as an institution. Right now, we are in a public relations battle, but it is a battle that we can win if we stay focused. I want to pass hunting down to future generations, to my children and my grandchildren. Understanding the motivations is the foundation that we can build upon to keep hunting a reality.

About the Author

Aaron B. Futrell is a lifelong hunter and angler from Canal Fulton, Ohio. He is currently the senior editor for The Hunting News. His articles and blogs focus on current events and the philosophy of hunting. He has a BA in History from The University of Akron and is a US Army veteran. You can learn more about Aaron and see more of his articles and hunting news commentary at thehuntingnews.com. You can also follow him on his Facebook page The Sportsman's Party.

Acknowledgments

I am thankful for the following people that made *Why We Hunt* possible.

Christina Futrell - Words cannot express my gratitude for the support you have given me throughout this entire process. Your patience and encouragement were paramount in this undertaking. You have stood by me from the beginning and I cannot imagine not having you in my life.

Ellen Ziegler - I want to thank you all for you time, incite and suggestions for making this book the best it could be.

Ray Futrell – Thank you for proof reading and offering your wisdom not only for this book, but for all you have giving me including life itself. You are an amazing father that I cannot thank enough.

Jonathon Sainsbury of 6x9 Design - You did a phenomenal job on the cover, thank you for your hard work and patience for dealing with a new author.

And last but not least I want to thank all of the hunters across this great land for inspiring me to write this book. Your love for the outdoors and passion should be an inspiration for all Americans.